EVERYTHING
PEOPLE

INDIA · SINGAPORE · MALAYSIA

Notion Press

No.8, 3rd Cross Street,
CIT Colony, Mylapore,
Chennai, Tamil Nadu – 600004

First Published by Notion Press 2020
Copyright © Ashfaq Syed 2020
All Rights Reserved.

ISBN 978-1-64899-905-5

EVERYTHING PEOPLE

A NEW ECONOMIC SYSTEM
FOR OUR FUTURE

ASHFAQ SYED

INDIA • SINGAPORE • MALAYSIA

INDICACADEMY

INDIC PLEDGE

———◆◆———

- *I celebrate our civilisational identity, continuity & legacy in thought, word and deed.*

- *I believe our indigenous thought has solutions for the global challenges of health, happiness, peace, and sustainability.*

- *I shall seek to preserve, protect and promote this heritage in doing so,*
  - *discover, nurture and harness my potential,*
  - *connect, cooperate and collaborate with fellow seekers,*
  - *be inclusive and respectful of diverse opinions.*

ABOUT INDIC ACADEMY

———◆◆———

Indic Academy is a non-traditional 'university' for traditional knowledge. We seek to bring about a global renaissance based on Indic civilizational and indigenous thought. We are pursuing a multidimensional strategy across time, space and cause by establishing centers of excellence, transforming intellectuals and building an ecosystem.

Indic Academy is pleased to support this book.

To my father, who is no more.

His Integrity and principles guide me throughout my life.

CONTENTS

Preface   *11*

Introduction   *19*

PART 1

1. New Economic System   33

2. People-Organizations for the New Economy   42

3. The New System Cooperatives   52

4. Support System for the People   63

5. Information Technology Tools   67

6. Local Community Service Centres   81

7. Collective Collaboration between Cooperatives   89

8. Work and Income in the New System   92

PART 2

9. IT and IT-Enabled Services   99

10. Food and Agriculture   102

11. Energy for Future   107

12. Manufacturing & Industries   110

13. Media   113

Contents

14. Transport & Travel   115

15. Education   124

16. Consumer Products and Services   133

17. Healthcare for All   136

18. Finance and Insurance   141

19. Real Estate & Construction   146

20. Legal-Justice for All   149

21. Sports and Games   152

22. Social and Public Sector   155

Conclusion   *161*

PREFACE

The world will not be the same again. COVID-19 has changed our lives forever. No doubt, unorganized daily-wage workers were suffering with a meagre sustenance for a long time, but the lockdown of COVID-19 broke their back and made them destitute. Workers who were sustaining for a long time on daily-wage work eating two meals with pride are now reduced to begging for food. This explains the exodus of migrant workers from large cities of India during the lockdown. They were willing to walk hundreds of kilometres, to be with their families rather than beg for food and die of hunger. The so-called food assistance programme making people stand in queue for hours together and the government machinery failing miserably to just provide food in an organized manner shows the complacency of the present economic system. The photo ops of politicians delaying the food to the needy are one of the examples, to what extent the political class can go to take advantage of the situation. When most of the unorganized workers left the cities, companies and government realized the importance of the work done by them and are now trying to devise plans to provide work, but I am sure it will not change anything. To solve this problem, the change should be drastic and moving forward; there should not a section of the society which would be called unorganized or gig-workers.

The middle-class has had a pretty good run in this capital-centric economy. Now they realize that they are also disposable and eventually lose their place in this system. It is high time they realize that they are part of 99% and not 1%. The system coerced them into unsustainable lifestyles which only made them go into debt rather than giving them a comfortable life. It made them believe in a lot of things which they thought mattered but, they do not matter at all. The virus and lockdown exposed the biggest scam perpetrated by the existing system, buying of unnecessary things on debt, like larger homes, shiny cars, designer dresses, latest mobile phones, travel to exotic places, etc. This lockdown has given us the incredible gift of a chance to introspect and rethink our entire life and economic life beyond the COVID-19 distress.

The blame-game going on around the world over who is responsible for COVID-19 distress is the sign of capitalists and the political class trying to walk away from their responsibilities. In the US blaming China and in India blaming a certain community are a few known distractions. This is not new, and every pandemic or distress is the time a blame-game starts and this are just distractions from the actual issue—why are we not prepared for these calamities? When we can prepare for wars with billions of dollars spent on fighter-planes, bombs, and guns, can't we have the infrastructure and equipment required to deal with a pandemic which can destroy the lives of millions? This is what happens when people are not in charge and not organized. Putting people first and smart organizing are the solutions provided in this book.

On the positive note, the abrupt disruption of the pandemic is what we required to make the drastic changes required to this unequal economic system. I started this book during the 2008 recession, and I was sure that the world was ready for this change but that did not happen. The impact was only to the poor and marginalized communities and not the entire system and also, the impact was cushioned by governments helping banks and financial institutions to resurrect the same system and it worked. Now, it is different. It has affected everyone and it's the right time to introspect and make the necessary changes. But, first a few things about myself.

I am not an economist but, an engineer with a master's degree in Industrial Engineering from Louisiana Tech University. My master's degree was all about designing systems and using technology to make them efficient. I did not work in pure Industrial Engineering per se but in the application of IE using Information Technology. In the course of my career, I worked in distribution management system for the food industry, highway construction management system for American Association for State Highway Transportation, Specimen Management System for Centres for Disease Control and many more around the world in my career of 25 years.

While developing those systems, I was not aware that in most cases, I was responsible for automating the work done by many employees and the companies simply removed them whenever the opportunity arose. A bloodbath occurred in one of the oil companies where I was consulting in 2007-08. An entire floor of employees was fired when the software I developed replaced their work. With so much blood on my hands, I started thinking about why the systems I develop are not helping people and only helping companies.

The year 2008-09 was the turning point where the companies and banks started collapsing. The corporate and bank bailout did resurrect the corporate world, people continued suffering, employees were laid off and the nightmare started for the people. Post the 2008-crash, with the bailout of culprit financial institutions without any consequence, was a case of pure crony capitalism. This is when I started thinking that capitalism has totally failed people and there is a need for a new economic system which works for people.

But, first, I wanted to see if the conclusions I have drawn are my own or that of most Americans (I was working in the US at that time). In August 2010, I wrote my first blog which was a letter from the American Consumers to the corporates, highlighting the frustration and disappointment of the American people with the corporates and the capitalist system itself. The blog got one hit in six years and that too from a guy who was trying to promote his own blog. I should admit that I did not do anything to promote the blog nor told anyone about it. So, the blog remained undiscovered for six years and I too had forgotten about it. However, I did not stop thinking about the new economic system and continued my research. Then, it happened; sometime in August 2016 an article appeared in none other than Wall Street Journal which was a letter from the Corporates to the American consumer asking what was wrong, why the consumers were not buying things at the same vigour like before and that they were saving more. It was as if the author was answering my blog and saying that the 2008-crash was the consumers' fault. This is when I decided that America and the world are ready for a new economic system.

My blog:

Thursday, August 26, 2010

Letter to the Corporations from an American Consumer

Dear Large Corporation,

This letter was long due and I finally took the time (thanks to you I have lots of time) to write this. Well, to start with, let us just go over the recent recession. It was bad. They called it 'great recession' for nothing. I was under the impression that we both were in it together and I did not find it odd that I lost my job at the first whiff of the recession. I also felt bad for you as some of you had to go and beg for hand-outs from the government (i.e., from me, the taxpayer) to survive the recession. I did not mind it as much, because I was sure that if you survive, I survive. You see, capitalism works that way: People build corporations, corporations make products, corporations give us jobs, and we buy those products and corporations grow bigger and create more jobs. The cycle was going on fine until you decided to break the cycle by yanking one major part of the chain, the jobs.

You conveniently got rid of me during the recession and when things were improving, you forgot to call me back. Instead, you got greedy and decided to hoard money in the bank. $1.5 trillion in the bank? That was not nice of you. What were you thinking? One thing you forgot: I am an employee and a consumer. Do you know what it means? I consume all the crap you make. Now, as an employee, I was getting money for my work and as a consumer, I was buying stuff. Do you see the problem? I have no job and no money, and I cannot buy your crap. Soon you may have to put all that stuff you are making, in the big hole down in the gulf.

Anyway, I am not writing this to make a truce or beg for my job. I am beyond making a truce. I was angry at first but, I have calmed down as it is difficult to think rationally when you are angry. Thanks to you for firing me as I have ample time to think and reflect on my consumer-life. All these years, everybody put me on the pedestal saying I am the most important part of the economy (70% important). The dream of corporations all over the world was to reach me through every possible communication medium. You made attractive ads on TV and radio, you sent me emails constantly and you even called me two-to-three times a day with attractive offers. I was pampered and in the last 20 years, except for a couple of years during what you called the cyclic recession, I have not disappointed you. For your information, even during the 2001-recession, when President Bush urged me to go and shop, I was there, taking whatever loans I could and doing my duty. But this recession is different. I not only lost my job, but I lost my house also. The constant source of money-flow I had (from the second, third mortgage) dried and the only hope I had was that, once the recession is over, you would recall me to my job and I can keep the wheels of the economy going again. But you betrayed me big-time and I have no choice but to take matters in my own hands. Don't worry; I am also going to tell you what I am going to do.

The first and foremost thing I will do is to stop paying my loans. It is nothing against you but, it is just strategic; you see, I need to survive first with mine and my family's basic needs and then think about the loans. It is not normal for me as I am doing this for the first time, but I learned from you. Why did you call it a 'strategic bankruptcy'? I know what you are going to say—'your credit will be toast'—well; I don't plan to take any loan or credit for a long time, so I am not worried about it. I will not apply for bankruptcy yet as I know how to play this game now. I know my rights and I know how to bring you to accept 10 cents on a dollar. Second, I will look around my life and see what I have, what I need and what I want. Even if I go with what I want, I am sure I don't need 50% of the stuff I have and the unnecessary buying will stop immediately. From now onwards, it will never be what 'you' think I want. Don't waste your money on ads as I will not be persuaded to buy anything I don't want. If you feel you still want to make ads, please make it funny so that at least it is entertaining.

You know what, I should thank you for doing this to me as I got time to think and reflect. It just hit me that, you are just recent phenomena and there was life without you earlier. Those were good old days when everything was local, and I was content in my life. All you have given me is grief and anxiety. Anyway, I know I will learn to survive without you but, unfortunately, you cannot survive without me. I know it is making you angry and I know that you are not going to quietly go away and also know that you are going to fight it with your conniving ways. I have only one thing to tell you: Bring it on!

The Reply after 6 years:

Dear American Consumer,

This is The Wall Street Journal. We're writing to ask if something is bothering you.

The sun shone in April and you didn't spend much money. The Commerce Department here in Washington says your spending didn't increase at all adjusted for inflation last month compared to March. You appear to have mostly stayed home and watched television in December, January and February as well. We thought you would be out of your winter doldrums by now, but we don't see much evidence that this is the case.

You have been saving more too. You socked away 5.6% of your income in April after taxes, even more than in March. This saving is not like you. What's up?

We know you experienced a terrible shock when Lehman Brothers collapsed in 2008 and your employer responded by firing you. We know stock prices collapsed and that was shocking too. We also know you shouldn't have taken out that large second mortgage during the housing boom to fix up your kitchen with granite countertops. You've been working very hard to pay off this debt and we admire your fortitude. But these shocks seem like a long time ago to us in a newsroom. Is that still what's holding you back?

Do you know the American economy is counting on you? We can't count on the rest of the world to spend money on our stuff. The rest of the world is in an even worse mood than you are. You should feel lucky you're not a Greek consumer. And China, well they're truly struggling there just to reach the very modest goal of 7% growth.

The Federal Reserve is counting on you, too. Fed officials want to start raising the cost of your borrowing because they worry they've been giving you a free ride for too long with zero interest rates. We listen to Fed officials all of the time here at The Wall Street Journal, and they just can't figure you out.

Please let us know the problem. You can reach us at any of the emails below. (Editor's Note: We asked, you answered.)

Sincerely,

The Wall Street Journal's Central Bank Team -By Jon Hilsenrath

It has been four years since this reply from the Wall Street Journal, and 12 years since the great recession and the stock market has gone up by leaps and bounds. This would give the impression that the economy of the world is doing very well.

There is no doubt that people world over are hurting economically and are in a dire situation. The capitalists are still trying to hold on to the system, on the premise that there is no revolution which would indicate their demise. In any other period, this same hurt would lead to revolution; however, the revolt will never come; because of the digital age, people have forgotten how to revolt. The people would vent their frustration on social media and go back to their life. This phase of decline will continue for a long period as the corporates will think of ways (through credit, etc.,) to keep it going.

During the COVID-19 distress, the corporates are not sitting quietly. In the US, they have already got their relief package. Airlines, cruises, hotels, restaurant chains, everyone got bailed out even while 30 million people applied for unemployment benefits. The small-relief-cheques are long gone, and I am sure most of the 99% are now in distress. But, one thing different from the 2008 crisis is that their life will not be the same again. The social distancing, job losses, China-blunder, etc. will definitely make way for the paradigm shift. This is the time to make the real change and take back the economy with a new economic system.

The first question to ask when we talk about the new system is the redundant stakeholders. In a capitalist system, with the automation, Information Technology and globalization, the workers are redundant. Many jobs which the workers used to do are automated and the workers become redundant. Since the workers are the consumers, two of the three stakeholders of the capitalist system are weakened. It is logical that capitalism cannot sustain without two of the three stakeholders. With this logic, another hypothesis can be drawn. With the advent of Information Technology which requires less capital to do the same job, do we need capitalistic corporates? In most sectors, we do not. If the workers can use the same Information Technology, the same systems and build and manage the collective cooperatives, we can restore all the stakeholders which are interlinked for the economic system.

One form of the socialist system was the one where the State owns most of the businesses and employing workers has been tried and failed. In this system, the capitalists are replaced by the State as the ruling elite and it is open to corruption and centralized control. There is a middle-ground possible where the best of both capitalism and socialism can be adopted and build a system, where capitalists are neutralized, and state corruption is removed.

This new system which would be a social democracy needs new kinds of organizations, collectives and cooperatives which are run democratically with the simple change where the corporate structure of **one-share-one-vote is replaced by one-person-one-vote** to effectively restore the harmony between the economic stakeholders. The economy also will be overturned from local-to-global rather than global-to-local.

The thesis of the book provides alternative possibilities, the organization structure and provides the process for the collectives and cooperatives to be established and managed democratically. Owning the technologies which would manage people's organizations, cooperatives would be the key to have an equitable system. In addition, it opens the mind of the youth to think about the possibilities which can emerge from this effort. The supporting technology platform is already built and ready to be deployed; just needs people to take it and run it.

INTRODUCTION

Even though the COVID-19 is the trigger which turned the system upside-down, the people around the world were hurting for a long time because of this unequal system. But, thanks to COVID-19, people got time during the lockdown to introspect. Many systems are disrupted at the root and the general conclusion is that life will not be the same again. However, the pain was there for people for a long time.

The economic inequality, in the last few decades, under capitalism has grown exponentially all over the world. Latest statistics show that the eight richest people in the world are worth as much as the bottom 50% of the world population i.e., 3.6 billion people. Is it due to capitalism? Yes, this inequality is inherent in capitalism which is skewed towards capitalists to accumulate wealth by a few. But there were external influences which accelerated given the automation in industries, Information Technology growth and globalization. It started with the consumerization and manufacturing growth in developed countries in the 80s and 90s. As the manufacturing and competition grew, the capitalists and industrialists wanted to make more money by reducing the cost which prompted the automation and outsourcing to low-wage countries instead of increasing the number of workers. This led to a jobless growth where the good jobs in manufacturing and services are lost and only the service-jobs which cannot be automated or outsourced remain.

This major step taken by the capitalists to automate and outsource was possible only due to the structure of the private companies. The one-share-one-vote concept of private enterprise concentrates the power at the top. The people with most shares decide the Board of Directors and the Board of Directors takes care of the major shareholders' interest, sacrificing the interests of the small investors as well as the workers. When the corporate interest is dictated by the major shareholders, and the major shareholders are happy only if the company makes money, the management-goal would be to find ways to reduce cost and increase profits. Also, the CEO and upper management want the piece of the pie when they devise strategies to increase profits. The CEOs' pay which is 300 times the average worker's pay in the USA reflects this nexus. There is absolutely no incentive for the CEOs to consider the welfare of workers when cheaper alternatives in terms of automation and cheaper outsourcing options are available.

The victims of the vicious cycle of increasing profits by corporates were the workers. The more automation was used, the fewer workers were required and if they still saw dissatisfied workers, it was better for them to take the manufacturing to low-wage countries. This did not mean a better life for workers in the outsourced countries, but, extremely low wages were paid and, in many cases, without regulations meant child-labour was being used. It was proudly accepted that the only goal of a private enterprise is to make money. Any steps taken by the enterprise towards the goal is the right step, otherwise, you are moving away from the goal. Naturally, the better wages demanded by the workers would take the company away from its goal.

In the service sector, even though the jobs vanished, the work which these workers did not vanish; instead, it was passed on to the customers which can be seen in consumers being their own travel agents, bank teller, checkout clerk, etc., without getting paid. The automation and technology which increased the efficiency and profitability of corporations did not trickle down to the consumers but, increased the profitability of the top management and investors. This skewed business-model and economy are unsustainable as the income and wealth keep flowing upwards and most of the people will be left behind. With this trend, we can safely say that the capitalism is not working for 99% of the people and there is a need for a new system which is more equitable and serves most people, not just the top 1%.

To develop the new system, it is important to analyze what went wrong and how to avoid those mistakes moving forward. It is interesting to see that the reasons for the collapse of capitalism are the tools which are necessary to build the new much-equitable system.

There are several reasons for the demise of capitalism. The top four reasons are:

1. The industrial automation

2. Information Technology

3. Globalization

4. Knowledge-economy

The Industrial automation

The industrial automation was in a way essential as the volume of products increased and the quality requirement was extremely high. The routine jobs where it was possible to have human error would be automated, but, the automation produced more products with the same amount of workforce or if the efficiency doubled, the workforce may not increase as per the efficiency increase but, at least may be 20 to 30%. Henry Ford, the owner of Ford motor company realized in the early years that paying workers more than other companies was more profitable to the company as the workers who worked at the plant can afford the cars he made. This fundamental reality is what the present-day companies and the capitalists forgot. The workers are the most loyal customers for a company. By eliminating the workers, you are basically eliminating the very loyal customers as well as spokespersons for the company. As in many cases, the companies took the automation to the highest level wherein, most of the workers were eliminated. This would be the beginning of the end for capitalism. When an important member of the economic cycle is removed, especially, when the member (worker) is also the customer (who is another big part of the economic cycle), the system will collapse. This is what is seen in developed countries where the industrial revolution started and moving to other countries which are following the footsteps of these countries.

The remedies to correct the course of capitalism from the effects of automation would have been several at the right time, but none of them was considered which led to the decline. The possible remedies would have been,

1. Recognize the important role the workers played in the growth of their industry both as worker-spokesperson of the company and as a loyal customer of the products

2. Share the efficiency gains from the automation with the workers and customers.

3. Community development effort as part of their corporate social responsibility

4. Contribute to the rehabilitation and skill-development of the laid-off workers

5. And finally caring about the people and not having the only goal of making money.

Globalization

The globalization was a double whammy for the workers from industrial countries where automation had displaced many jobs. This was the biggest blow to workers as the companies just picked up and left for cheaper labour around the world. It is to be noted that the developing country workers did not benefit much as the factories have become sweatshops exploiting the labour by paying them low wages in extremely pathetic working conditions. It is also interesting to know that the direct labour cost in most of the manufacturing companies is 6 to 10% of the total cost. The inventory and material cost is 55 to 60%. As an industrial engineer in charge of reducing the cost, I would suggest the company to reduce cost from materials and inventory rather than eliminating jobs. If the labour cost is reduced by 50% by moving production to China, the total cost-reduction will be 3 to 5% when the material cost is almost the same anywhere in the world. Also, the saving will further have reduced taking into consideration the transportation and logistics cost when the finished goods are brought back to the country bringing the savings to only about 1 to 2%. However, if the material and inventory cost is reduced by just 10% through material research and reducing inventory, the overall cost saving will be around 6%. The globalization did not improve the bottom-line of the companies but, by eliminating workers, they eliminated most loyal customers. This is the second biggest mistake made by the corporations which led to the decline of capitalism.

The globalization if utilized in the right way, would have been a wonderful opportunity for everyone in the world. The right way would have been:

1. Export the expertise developed over several decades to the developing countries, not the jobs.

2. Replicating the production systems in other countries (not moving) to help their economy as well as making a profit would not harm anybody.

3. Remove the corporate creed of only making money and replace with sustainable growth keeping all the stakeholders together.

4. Ethical globalization which does not harm people is the only sustainable business-model.

Information Technology

Information Technology accelerated the demise as it changed the whole business-model and business structure. Many people believe that Information Technology itself is not a sector like manufacturing or finance, etc. because it is just a tool to streamline the operations in other sectors. For example, the banks had a system of handling money (deposit/withdrawal or making a loan, etc.,) before the software was developed to replicate exactly the banking system to make it more efficient. The efficiency allowed banks to cater to more customers with the same number of employees. The manual system where ten employees could handle up to 1000 accounts, turned into a system where the same employee could handle 100,000 customers. If the cost of a physical bank branch transaction costs $10, the ATM, online or mobile transaction would cost less than $1; the more customers did transactions outside the branch, the more profits the banks made. The best part was that the software once developed could be used multiple times at multiple places without additional cost. This IT revolution spreading to each sector made more and more professions obsolete like the travel agents, bankers, etc. More than industrial automation and globalization, the IT revolution is responsible for more displacement of workers and contributing to the demise of capitalism. The IT could have been a catalyst in improving the lives of the whole humanity but, instead, was used to profit a few and contribute to the massive inequality.

Knowledge-economy

The knowledge-economy requires human capital rather than financial capital compared to the industrial economy. The last few decades of the industrial economy unknowingly started the transition into a knowledge-based economy, but, without taking along the most important stakeholders, that is, the people. The capital moved into automation, Information Technology and IT-Enabled Services leaving the industrial workers behind. This showed in the western economy with huge income-gap between capital income and wages. The capital was applied where there is absolutely no requirement of it. The new-age companies in the knowledge-economy (mostly in IT) exploited the high valuations in a fragile business-model where the only tangible assets are their employees. It can be noted that the capitalism is trying to play the same game in marginalizing the important stakeholders, the people, as they did in industries but, it does not work as the workers in this economy walk out with the knowledge and can create the same type of company or better without much effort. However, the larger companies with huge investor funds crushed the small companies and concentrated the wealth among the top 1%. The top 100 IT entrepreneurs in the US have a net worth of $1 trillion.

The new economic system

The new system should consider the present situation and reverse the trend of wealth-flow to the top to be more equitable to the 99% of the people economically. This is easier than most people think and is possible only because of the automation and IT revolution. The systems I built for the companies to become efficient and helped them to lay-off employees are the tools which will help us build the new system. The only thing is that we need to own these automation and IT tools. Also, we cannot be individuals and expect the systems to help us. The following steps are required to change the system.

1. Never be an individual, organize

2. Change the structure of the companies from capitalist-centric (private) to people-centric (cooperative)

3. Change worker income just-from-work to compensation-from-work, dividend compensation from cooperatives and social security benefits.

4. Utilize IT, automation, and globalization benefit to people instead of corporates

5. Move from competition to a shared economy

6. Take control of the democracy

Organize

The first and foremost step now is for people to organize. Back in 1971, the infamous secret Powell memo to the Chamber of Commerce kick-started the associations for the corporate sector. "Without organization, corporate rights and interests cannot be protected," said Powell. This initiated several corporate think-tanks, every possible trade associations and lobbying firms were created in the next few years making it the biggest cause of the separation of workers from the capital. There is even a trade association for parking-lot owners. These organizations cater to only corporations, businesses and organizations but, none of them accepts individual memberships. 'NONE OF THEM ACCEPT INDIVIDUAL MEMBERSHIPS', there is a reason for that, the companies want us to be individuals and not organized which is a big threat to them. If one consumer complains about the product or service provided by the corporation, they do not want anybody else to know about it. If there is a disgruntled employee or worker, they want to deal with only that person instead of a union or an association. It is ironic that every small, medium and large corporation has associations but, for people, they want us to be individual. Individualism perpetrated by Ayn Rand is the Bible for many politicians and the corporate bigwigs but, they are the ones who have support systems built for them to have a collective voice. It is time to have associations of people to have a collective voice for everything. No matter what the belief system is for different people, but, it is important that the people join and make their voice heard. In fact, that is what the corporates are counting on, to keep us as individuals and can divide and rule. The organization or associations are the modern-day representation of people. Be it the government we elect, Jobs we do, or products and services we use and access, we should be part of a group or association to exercise our rights and find our voice. The vicious cycle of corporate and government nexus should stop, and people's needs and wishes should be the foremost goal for any country.

There are many IT tools (Phapa organization management system), online fora, and social networks available which allow people to organize. These tools allow an organization or a group to rapidly grow from single-digit members to millions.

Corporations to cooperatives

The basic structure of 'one-share-one-vote' in the corporation articles of association which created the whole mess we see in the capitalism. If one-person-one-vote was used, every shareholder, no matter how many shares he has, would have the same rights and if the workers or employees were given part of the compensation as shares, there wouldn't be any accumulation of power and wealth in hands of few. Incidentally, 'one-person-one-vote' is the basic structure of a cooperative and these are the entities which would replace the corporation in the new system.

The cooperatives have played a very important role in service economies and aptly suited for knowledge-economy due to its very structure, where, the capital and workers are the same. The private corporations were required in industrial sectors where huge capital was required, however, the corporations have no role in people-centric organizations.

The cooperatives are democratic organizations with one-person-one-vote concept no matter how much capital or shares they have. The members and shareholders decide on the services to provide, workers to hire and profit-sharing. The cooperatives work like a private business but, with a small difference, in which, the private business, the biggest shareholder dictates what needs to be done. Also, the one with a similar structure but, being small, the cooperative cannot compete in efficiency, cost and technology. The present cooperatives are suitable for small businesses at the local level. However, the Everything-People cooperative model is the 21st-century cooperative model, which is a social business, efficient, cost-effective and scalable using the technology and automation.

In this book, only a few sectors are covered for deep analysis and solutions. But, with the evolution of the new system, most of the sectors can be transformed into cooperative businesses and help in redistribution of income and wealth to help everyone.

Utilize IT & and automation to our advantage

Information Technology touches every person and every sector. IT will be the first people's organization needed to jump-start the economic system. If we want to reverse the trend of trickle-down system, we need to own IT. IT sector is the one which does not need the financial capital an industrial sector needs but, it has been projected as if it does. Imagine the returns on a one-million-investment in the industrial sector will be 20% at the most and same investment will produce one billion dollars in IT sector. This is only because the IT sector needs human capital, not financial capital. As an IT technologist working in IT for the last 20 years, I can tell you that it is the biggest scam perpetrated on the world. It is rife with buzz words, unnecessary upgrades and meaningless features and the IT sector gets away with it. This has been the hallmark of IT in the past 20 years. You will learn that software has 20% features you need and 80% bullshit. Also, you may think, it is too late to veer the course when the companies have become monster multi-nationals, but, this is the one industry where the David-and-Goliath-story holds. Think about it; you as one person can have a digital business up and running in one week. You can set up and run a call-centre in a day. You can do most of the IT work from home but, it would take one year and huge capital to set up a small manufacturing unit. So, it is not too late, and it is the best time for people to take control.

So, we are going to learn, the areas where it is easiest to take it first and how the entire sector can be moved to people's control. With this exercise, 20% of the total jobs will be created in the IT and IT-Enabled Services sector. People will be spending 30-to-40% less on IT-related products and services. 60% of the cost of education will be reduced across-the-board and the only people who enjoy working in IT will be the ones working in this field. Every country will have a nationwide association of IT and ITES Workers. A nationwide cooperative will develop and manage software, applications and mobile apps required to run every industry, department and every entity. A nationwide ITES cooperative will provide support through call-centres, back-office for every industry and every sector.

Moving from Competition to shared economy

The competition in capitalism was supposed to improve the quality of products and services for the consumers, provide the consumers' choices and remove monopoly, but, instead, the corporations were so engrossed in making money, that the goal is to manipulate, collude and disfranchise the consumers and workers. Since in most cases, consumers and workers are the same, elimination of one hurts the other. The so-called competition was just eyewash and the companies manipulated the public perception through predatory advertisements and adding features to the products and services which have no value-addition to the consumers. It has come to the point where the company which makes the best advertisement is considered to have the best product. The people end up becoming the victims of the manipulations and end up buying unwanted crap products again and again. Even though most of the people know this, they are not able to do anything about it. This destructive trend has to change, and we should move to a shared economy where we buy only things which we need and have different quality-scales in which we have to have our own standards which the companies, products and services should abide before we buy.

The shared economy is the most eco-friendly, healthy and cost-effective for people. The new system should be designed to organize and decide which products we need to buy and share.

Taking back democracy

The recent trend around the world in electing right-populist governments is a symptom of the people struggling and this fear and desperation are being exploited by the populist organizations. These right-wing populist political parties and corporates together have seized power. The economic struggle of people during this populist government and crony capitalism is worse than at any time in the past.

Now with Covid-19, the incompetency of these governments is visible for everyone and people are introspecting and the influence of private corporations on the government is quite evident everywhere and people have been sidelined, manipulated and disfranchised in the very pinnacle of people's movement which is democracy. The very core of this income-inequality is the influence the rich and the corporations have on the election and democracy. The corporate-favoured policies and destruction of welfare to the poor and needy during this COVID-19 is visible to everyone. India saw an exodus of migrant workers willing to travel by walking, cycling, packed in tankers just to get away from this destitute situation. The US saw almost 30 million people apply for unemployment benefits and the loans meant for small and medium businesses were gobbled up by big corporations. These are all the signs that capitalism is collapsing, and the governments controlled by these crony capitalisms should go for the new system to work.

So, what can be done to take back the democracy and government from the clutches of these predatory influences? Again, the answer lies in the first principle—Organize. Without being a collective, there is nothing we can do. The divide-and-rule has been their strength and also, corrupt politicians' nexus with the corporates has to be broken. One basic question each one of us needs to ask ourselves is why the corporation should participate in any election by funding political parties when democracy is all about people.

PART 1

1

New Economic System

The wealth-flow from 99% to the 1% is not an accidental phenomenon, but a coordinated effort which happened over the last 40 years. As the corporates organized themselves into groups based on all different sectors and represented themselves, their efforts bore fruit with most of the benefits through government laws completely flowing to the top. It was easy to skew the system towards the corporations and the rich as they were well organized, well-funded and well-connected in the government. Along with this skewed conventional business-model, another greater threat appeared in the form of internet-based businesses. The conventional businesses at least had some human requirement in physical infrastructure setup, construction and managing the business but, the internet business eliminated even those possibilities. An internet business further reduced the need for people and killed completely the conventional service industry. A billion-dollar business would need less than 100 people to manage whereas a business of the same size would employ thousands of people. The case in point: Today, Amazon market cap is bigger than Walmart's.

It is important to know what exactly these internet-based companies do compare to conventional business. They simply take the conventional business online. Instead of selling things in retail stores, the online store sells things over the internet or mobile. Instead of purchasing tickets at the local travel agent, you buy tickets online right from home. This business-model allowed internet-based companies to expand rapidly around the world at a fraction of the cost of normal business expansion. After tasting blood, every sector business went online: banking, travel, healthcare, education, energy, retail and even food purchase. This model literally increased the profitability of companies exponentially at the cost of employment to people. The recent upswing in the use of mobile phones and automation will even further reduce the need for workers and employees further alienating people from economic growth. It is also significant to note that, even though the capital requirement of the internet companies was a fraction of the conventional business, a huge capital flowed into these companies anticipating a windfall from the global business prospects.

The notion that internet companies have an innovative business-model is a farce and the capitalists who poured billions into these companies have been drumming this to justify and protect their investment. However, the reality is that these companies have a very fragile business-model which can be reproduced by anyone with knowledge of software programming along with the people who have worked in that field. This is the biggest advantage people have today. We do not need capitalists in any shape or form to establish and run an internet-based or mobile-based company. Even the conventional banks are encouraging customers to do their transactions online or through mobile and would charge a fee if they do the same transaction at the physical bank. The largest bank in India gave the real reason for this change. A transaction done inside the bank costs the bank Rs.65, an ATM transaction costs Rs.12 and an online transaction costs just Rs.2. It is fair that they want to reduce the cost by moving people online to transact. But it is to be noted that when people used to transact at the bank, the banks still made huge profits. However, with customers doing their business online and the bank saving anther Rs.63 per transaction, they would increase their profits exponentially. Imagine the same transaction is carried out in a cooperative bank where the customers and the workers are the shareholders. The Rs.63 would not go to the rich shareholders and top executives of the bank but to the customers and workers. The new system should use the same business-model of reducing the cost through the use of technology but, the profit from this business-model should go to the workers and customers.

How can the new economic system reverse the trend and make sure that the benefits are internalized to the people rather than the corporates and their shareholders? For this to happen, we require a whole new type of people's organizations, collectives and cooperatives which will systematically reverse the trend. Fortunately, there are many pieces of the new system that already exist which are suppressed by the corporates to make them ineffective; however, it is the easiest way to revive these entities and build the new system.

This paradigm shift from the corporate-centric to people-centric requires a framework which provides the necessary organizational structure for it. The structure expands from local to state, national and global. Many of the ingredients are already there and just need to recognize them and expand them. Major misgivings of the local businesses which are people-centric are that local businesses are inefficient, expensive and wasteful, whereas global corporations are efficient, cheaper and reduce waste. Well, presently, they are right, but, with the new paradigm, the local businesses will have the support and knowledge-base and the technology to be efficient, cheaper and profitable.

The framework for the Everything-People System starts with recognizing the stakeholders in it: the people who invest, the people who make and provide product and services and the people who use it. The corporates had the same stakeholders but, having only one goal of making money made them ignore the other major stakeholder—the people who are workers making the products and services and alienated the other stakeholders who are also the people who use them. This model takes care of all the stakeholders in a way it should be.

The Everything-People System starts with the creation of organizations, collectives and networks for each segment in the new economic system. The networks spanning local, state and country would be managed by sector-specific experts and Information service providers who would provide the services with the sponsorship of the social network.

Ingredients of the new economic System

The ingredients of the new economic system are:

- ◆ People are organized. Everyone is part of one or the other people-organizations

- ◆ The system is people-centric and not capital-centric

- ◆ Will go from local-to-global rather than global-to-local

- ◆ Driven by technology. But technology owned by people

- ◆ Company structure to be cooperative rather than private companies

- ◆ Local community service centres

People-Organizations

The concept of individualism should be the first thing which needs to be eliminated to participate in the new system. Even though we do most of the things in groups, the capitalist system prefers us to be individuals so that they can take advantage of it. However, the corporates themselves have realized the advantage of being in a group even when they are competing. For example, the airline industry has several associations and alliances among themselves to swing laws in their favour, cut costs, improve service and increase profits. If they are alone, no lawmaker listens to them. Too much competition will kill their business resulting in higher overheads and lower profits. However, they want people to be individuals so that we do not have a voice.

If an individual has a complaint against the airline, it will be a big process to just register the complaint. The ordeal of calling the customer service and getting nowhere is well-known. Also, the airline will make sure that no one else will know about the complaint. Do we have an alternative? Create consumer organizations. The organization should be well-funded; it should have customer-support, technology to manage the organization and should make a concerted effort with specific goals to achieve the required result from it.

One more example of people-organization is schools' Parent-Teacher Association. It should be established and managed specifically to make sure that all aspects of the students' welfare are taken care of. The association should not be confined to the school but should extend from the school to district, state and national levels. The same principle applies to every sector both social as well as economic.

People-centric rather than capital-centric

In the present-day corporate businesses, there is hardly any capital invested by the investors. Most of the investment is debt from banks. The workers are hired on a contract basis; they procure the technology and automation required with the borrowed money and if the business succeeds, the management and so-called investors make money. If the business fails, they declare bankruptcy and run away leaving huge loans to the bank and depositors. Well, with this unstable system, only people lose their deposits and suffer silently. If only we had an organization of depositors and part of the decision-making process in the banks, none of these delinquents would get loans and bankers would be behind bars if they commit frauds.

So, when there is no capital investment in capitalistic businesses, where is capitalism? There is only a last structure standing weak. It is time to give the last push and people-centric organizations should take over. The cooperatives' failure in India is also due to the hierarchical structure created because of the lack of knowledge about the cooperatives and their principles. Most of the cooperatives are owned mostly by politicians with fictitious members and no accountability. The true people-centric cooperative organizations would be owned by people and using technology and automation, will be able to succeed in any business.

Local-to-global rather than global-to-local

The globalization in the 1980s and 1990s was defined by the outsourcing of services to the countries with low labour cost. We learned in our industrial subjects that in cost of production, the direct cost of labour is only 6–10%. To save 10% of the cost, you would travel thousands of miles and ship the products back at an enormous cost.

The countries are importing and exporting food products around the world. The global multinational companies help this process and the food would travel hundreds of kilometres before reaching the plate. But most of this travel is unnecessary. The multinational companies benefit enormously from these transactions but, the value-added is minimal. One company would be exporting food products from one country to many countries. And another company would be importing the same type of products from different countries to the same country which was exporting its produce.

If we look at the requirement of the local economies from the local producers, this problem will not arise, and the trend can be reversed. The idea of choice perpetrated by global corporates is preposterous. No one will aspire to eat Washington apples in Patna, India when we have a more than sufficient produce of apples available in India itself. If it is done rationally, the local requirement is fulfilled first and then the remaining would be exported.

The local food requirement fulfilled by local producers is the best place to start. Food is one thing everyone needs and with the COVID-19 disrupting the supply chain, this is the best time to reverse the trend and make the local first and move to the state, countrywide and international as required, instead of global first. India has many cooperatives which are related to food and these cooperatives should be provided with the technology to fulfil the demand locally and reverse the trend.

The system driven by technology and technology owned by people.

I cannot stress enough about using technology for our benefit. When there is an option to book a ticket from home using technology i.e., website and app, that is the best way rather than standing in a queue at the railway station. If people are not able to do this, there should be a support system which helps them do it. Under no circumstances should people be standing in a queue and be helpless. This helps people to save time, money, and hassle. You may ask what happens to the ticket collector who will lose his job. Yes, he does lose his job but, there will be two jobs created for back-office support-people helping people booking tickets over the phone or online booking fees. The only catch is people (through cooperatives) own the technology which helped in booking online. If the technology is owned by a company, the ticket collector will lose his job, there are no support-people helping and the entire booking fee will go to the large corporation which owns the technology—technology used in online-only businesses owned by private companies are more of a threat to people than other types of business.

A Walmart store takes years to build and start a business. An online website takes a few weeks or days to build and start the operation. How can these two compete? Technology has disrupted many business models causing the biggest job losses. Every sector is sort of a victim or beneficiary of the Info-Tech revolution depending on which side you are. The capitalists are rejoicing over the rapid development in technology. With this, they can reduce the cost to a fraction and can run the business with very few employees compared to brick-and-mortar companies. And they are able to expand worldwide in a few months. However, workers in all sectors from manufacturing to finance are suffering. The workers have realized that workers' cooperatives are the answer to the job losses, but they do not seem to understand that these cooperative models do not work unless the technology is used. It is like fighting with a sword when the enemy has a machine-gun. The technology should be used effectively to build cost-effective and efficient cooperative businesses.

Owning the technology is easier than people think. Also, it is not a big mystery that only a few programmers are required to develop these technologies and own it. The new economic system will bring together these technologists and programmers and develop these required technologies for the new system for the people.

Businesses should be Cooperative-based rather than private companies.

The large corporations with their only goal to make money would run their business with the minimum workforce and price their products to maximize their profits. This is their inherent structure. The decision-making also is in the hands of a few people and the decision to use technology outsource to low-wage countries can be taken very easily.

But, when we see the industry structure of a country and the benefits to people of a country, we see the glaring inequalities.

For example, an industry which is, say, 10% of the GDP. It means that 10 % of the revenue is made by that industry's companies and businesses working in that industry. Now, if only 1% of the population is working directly or indirectly in that industry, that means, if the industry is making 10 billion dollars, only 1 billion goes to the people and 9 billion goes to the corporates and their investors. Do you see the problem? This is how inequality grows. You need not be an economist to understand it.

Imagine that the same corporations in that industry were cooperatives. Owned by people and managed by people, the entire 10 billion would go to the people, i.e., shareholders of the cooperative business. The cooperative business may be managed by the same MBAs and technologists but, the only difference is that while the corporate business is owned by a few shareholders who may not have anything to do with the business and make money just by investing borrowed money, in the cooperative business the shareholders are the actual stakeholders like workers, employees or customers.

The new economic system will base its entire economic system on cooperative business rather than large private companies.

Local community service centres

'Online-only' business has no relevance in the new system. Online is just one form of purchasing goods and services. It is true that online-only business has reduced the cost of products, but how will people buy products if they do not have jobs? It is important to understand that online companies do not produce any products and it is simply a tool for people to purchase products or services through the internet or mobile. But, if the purchased product requires servicing, it is an ordeal to send it back to the online retailer and get it repaired. What if there is a way to have a system where the delivery of the product is done through a local centre and purchased product is serviced locally? It creates jobs locally, gives confidence for people to buy online and helps the local economy to grow. The local service centres do just that.

The common local service centres will be the face of all the products and services purchased online. Also, for many types of services provided locally like banking, bill payments, delivery, healthcare and education services etc., the service centre can be one-room-operation or a large multi-purpose place.

2

PEOPLE-ORGANIZATIONS FOR THE NEW ECONOMY

My biggest frustration over the years has been being cheated by US corporations through their conniving business practices. The cable companies and their one-month free HBO activated without my consent or knowledge and then kept charging for it until I realized it, sometimes months later as I had auto-pay on, the mobile phone companies when they had contracts and complicated minutes' plans, then there were banks with their automatic enrolment into overdraft facilities and the exorbitant fees... These were not isolated incidents but, just a few of the many of conniving business plans cooked up to deceive people and make more money. When I mention it to my friends or colleagues about it, they would say "Yes, it happened to me also" but, they would add "What to do, next time I have to be careful." None of them would consider it cheating and everyone would say, it is their fault as they should have been careful.

It was not this way in the 1990s decade when I first moved to the US. The customer service was the best and customers were treated with so much care and it was awesome. I remember when I used to call the customer-support number, a real person would answer and would solve our problem immediately. If the problem was complicated, she would put me on hold to consult with her superiors and come back and in most cases, give the solution in the customer's favour. I remember in 1996, when the rental car broke down at my house, just as I was leaving for work, I called the rental company and they said they will fix it. A little over 20 minutes later, there was a knock on the door and a guy from the rental company was standing with a pad and a form to sign. He had come in a tow-truck with a car on top of it. He said he had already loaded the stalled car and showed me the brand-new car standing in my driveway as my replacement car. My father was visiting from India and he could not believe the kind of service they gave and had a great story to tell back home. I move to India in 2000 for a few years and would all the time, compare the pathetic customer service in India with the wonderful service in the US.

However, when I returned to the US in 2005, things had changed drastically. The customer service was non-existent. It was normal to wait over the phone for one hour for a customer-support person (mostly from India) and literally, none of our problems would be solved favouring me, the customer. The Corporations' plan was simple; as an individual, I was isolated. Most of us wouldn't know that they are being cheated; some of us would realize it and blame themselves for not being careful and a fraction of us would take the pain to call and complain. It is a number game; 90% would not realize it, 9% realize it and blame themselves and 1% are trouble-makers; so, the trouble-makers should be frustrated by long waits on customer service calls and when finally, 'online' assures them that it will be solved and then does nothing. If we are individuals, they do not have to bother at all. An individual, the one-percent trouble-makers, who am I going to tell? There is no organization; I am not part of a group. The business-model I thought had changed from 'survival of the fittest to survival of the meanest'. The airlines, cable companies, banks, phone companies, everyone had changed. It seemed like they all had joined together and schemed to cheat the customers. Wait a minute; that is exactly what they did.

The infamous Powell memo kick-started the corporate takeover of the world. Back in 1971, the infamous secret Powell memo to his neighbour in Chamber of Commerce kick-started the associations for the corporate sector. 'Without organization, corporate rights and interests cannot be protected' said Powell. This initiated several corporate think-tanks, every possible trade association and lobbying firm was created in the next few years making it the biggest cause of the separation of workers from the capital. There is even a trade association for parking-lot owners. These organizations cater to only corporations, businesses and organizations, but none of them accepts individual memberships. There is a reason for that; the companies want us to be individuals and not organized which is a big threat to them. If one consumer complains about the product or service provided by the corporation, they do not want anybody else to know about it. If there is a disgruntled employee or worker, they want to deal with only that person instead of his union or association. It is ironic that every small, medium and large corporation has associations but, for people, they want us to be individual. Individualism perpetrated by Ayn Rand is the Bible for many politicians and the corporate bigwigs, but they are the ones who have support systems built for them to have a collective voice.

It is time to have associations of people to have a collective voice for everything. No matter what the belief system is for different people, it is important that the people join and make their voice heard. In fact, the corporates are counting on, keeping us as individuals so that they can divide and rule. The organization or associations are the modern-day representation of people. Be it the government we elect, Jobs we do, or products and services we use and access, we should be part of a group or association to exercise our rights and find our voice. The vicious cycle of corporate and government nexus should stop, and people's need and wishes should be the foremost goal for any country.

What kinds of organizations are required now? Unions are so 20th century. I am not degrading the unions but, I am giving the 21st-century version. In this version, there are no us and them (i.e., workers and investors), there are no negotiations for higher wages or jobs, but, an equal partnership where everyone has the same rights. The humiliation of begging for jobs, higher wages or working conditions will stop. We, the people would dictate the way the companies should run, and companies are managed. When the shift from financial capital to human capital happens, there are no billion-dollar executive salaries and bonuses. There are no acquisition costs and marketing costs for acquiring customers. When the customers and the employees are the investors, we decide what products and services we want and from whom we get it.

Our representatives in government are not fulfilling the peoples' mandate and carrying out the corporate agenda, this is a big problem. When the corporations violate rules of law, it is important to prevent these problems rather than solve it later. How can we do it? By organizing. This does not mean that people should be on the street in protest (again a 20ᵗʰ-century option) but, we do it by organizing and making the right decisions before it happens. Take the example of the US elections; with the election of Donald Trump, it is either that the people's choice was ignored completely, or the majority of Americans are racists. My money is on the first one where the American voter was thrust with the two worst candidates and the best among the worst won. It should have not come to that at all. The American people have forgotten that they are electing a person to represent them, not to rule on them.

This catastrophe would have been avoided if only the American people had a voice. This will change dramatically when people are organized. In fact, the first area of organizing should be in electing the representative government. It may seem like there are two contrasting views between the two major parties in the US, but deep down, people want good-paying jobs, a decent lifestyle, good education, etc.

To create the representative government, the first and foremost step would be to create an organization of people with common goals and aspirations.

It is important to know people who like to work in government are representatives. That starts with the right education. The education in this field is not when you start in the field but, way before when they complete education and start a career. That is right, being a government representative is a career and it should be treated like that; instead, they are becoming kings and queens and rule over the people. Imagine the system where the people's organization of voters decides on the manifesto, the policy of how the government should work and then elect the representatives from within the organization. The system where you choose a leader should stop and should choose a representative.

The notion of individualism, individual needs and wants are created by the corporates and capitalists to divide and rule. The very definition of a human being is that we are social animals. That means, we live in groups and collectively. It is against human nature to be individuals. If any of the needs and wants of people as individuals are compared, it will match with a group most of the time. If an individual wants a TV for entertainment, there are millions of people with the same need. So, in the new system, there is no individualism and no individual needs but, collective needs. This also does not mean that people will be forced to be part of a group which they do not belong to: for example, a group of parents whose children are going to a school or a school district or a broader group at state and centre-level. Another example is the support group with a disease like diabetes; with this group, you are not alone anymore. You get support and information about the disease; you contribute to the group with information, get the best treatment with the lowest cost and buy related medicine at low cost. In the same example, if you want to exercise your individualism and do everything by yourself, you are doing your own research in getting the information about living with the disease, paying a lot more for the same treatment and drugs. This is true in many situations in our daily life. From living in a grouped subdivision and apartment complex to accessing different services, the group is most suitable than the individual. Individualism complicates life and groups simplify life. There are more collective business models which are being touted by the same corporations but with only the intention to make more money. In the new system, the organizations which are created by groups of people based on different needs would help only people rather than corporates.

Using social network technology, the groups can be created based on several criteria like products and services accessed, work-related, social, cultural affiliations and many more. The parent-teacher associations are there in every school in America, but they are limited to only particular schools. In the new system, the PTAs should be extended to school districts, state and country-level. The decisions taken by elected officials at state and federal level affect every parent, teacher and child in the country. If the elected official believes in privatizing education and abolishes public education, there is no one organization which can protect the interests of the children. During the 2008 recession, when all the big banks were bailed out, the states and local governments cut funding for public schools. One school district in Georgia reduced the number of buses and routes which effected many rural children going to school. The parents were furious, but they could not do anything. The protests were limited to the school-level, but the school administration was helpless. If there was a PTA at the school, district, state and federal level, there was no way this could have happened when it affected so many children.

The new system organizations are not only meant for reactive action but, for proactive action. Any school, school board, state and federal education department should represent and serve the needs of the students. With the organization pro-actively making sure what most of the stakeholders want, that is what should happen in administration. This is the basic principle of democracy which has been forgotten in many countries.

Proactive organizations serve another very important role. Pick the companies which serve our interest and put the others to rest. When I mentioned about the golden period of the 1990s for customer service, one significant difference was less number of competitors. Competition is important, but too much competition is bad for customers. For example, back in those days, only three companies were in the telecom business in the US; they did not have to do cutthroat competition. They did compete by giving a lot of freebies for customers, but not by advertising the loudest on the TV. They also did it through good service; compare that to today: There are more than ten companies in the telecom business in each state. The more the companies, the more competition and collusion. The companies' association will make sure to lobby and make the laws favouring them and customers will pay more one way or the other. The companies which are going down due to competition do not go down without a fight; they will make sure they fight and they fight dirty. There are several sectors where there is too much competition like automobiles, airlines, electronics, etc., which are not adding any value to the consumers by giving us a choice.

The organizations also help us become customers for the local cooperatives, workers-owned as well as consumer-owned. The cooperatives will be discussed in the next chapter, but imagine the cooperatives owned by local people get ready customers without expensive marketing for customers. Acquisition of customers is the best way to beat the corporations which are eliminating jobs to make more money. The associations become the consumers and create thousands of local jobs using the saved advertisement and customer-acquisition cost.

So, the organizations which are required are based on the need of the people, but a comprehensive collective. If the organization or association is based on the type of work, there can be an association of knowledge, manufacturing, service or agriculture workers. If it is based on the type of sector, finance, insurance, healthcare, education transportation, energy, etc., should be created.

The ingredients for the organizations would be

1. Everyone will pay the fees to manage the organization
2. Professionally managed organizations with paid managers and employees
3. Give voice to each and everyone in the organization
4. Provide mentorship, education and tools required for learning and growth in the work
5. Shared and collective prosperity principle rather than individual
6. Access products and services as a group rather than individuals

The organizations required

1. Employee & Worker organizations
2. Community organizations
3. Consumer organizations
4. Social organizations.

5. Private member networks

6. Small business organizations.

7. Civic and consumer organizations

These organizations at local, state and central level ensure that no individual is left behind, and everyone's voice is heard. When the products and services are accessed from corporates, government, and any other sources it ensures that when it comes to choosing, they can make the right choice based on what is best for them rather than swayed by who makes better advertisements. These organizations will act as the first line of defence for the people to voice their concerns, complaints and problems. The organization's roles and responsibilities would be to:

1. Provide pertinent, unbiased and well-researched information required for the people to know about the entities they are dealing with as well as the products and services they are accessing

2. Create a database of information to be disseminated and accessed by the people

3. Negotiate and make agreements with the organization to get the best possible prices and support as a group rather than individuals for products and services

4. Be the conduit for the people to get support from the companies, government and organizations for complaints, concerns and problems

5. Facilitate the creation of new-age cooperatives and entities with people-centric goals rather than corporations which exist only to make money.

6. Acquire or create technologies required to run the cooperatives and other local entities most efficiently, cost-effectively, environment and people-friendly.

7. Make sure that most of the income and profit goes to the cooperative shareholders, workers and the consumers.

Example of the organization working for its stakeholders is in education, i.e., Parent-Teacher Association. The goal of the parents, as well as the teachers, is only in the best education and welfare of students. This applies to the schools where the students are children who are protected and helped by their parents and teachers. The school—whether government or private—does not matter if the students' welfare and education is the goal. The school is not the only place where decisions are made which affect the students. The local, district, state and central governments make the decisions and the association of parents and teachers should be extended to these government entities.

The example of the organization goals and purpose should be

1. Should work with a defined goal for the welfare of students at every level from school to national based on the goals and purpose at each level.

2. The goals and laws should always be debated and democratically decided before implemented with a specific time frame.

3. Should be the only authority to make the required changes in the school and government at every level. No corporates, no external influence.

4. The head of the government department of education should be a representative of this organization only.

5. Any school whether private or public (government) should be monitored by this organization to make sure of the compliance.

6. All purchasing of books, uniforms and any other related products and services should be done through the cooperatives.

7. The management of the school should have a major representation in this organization.

8. The private school and government school budget should be controlled by the management with major representation from this organization.

9. Like the staff, the organization's representatives should be trained to perform their duty of representing the organization and their goals.

10. The representative job should always be a paid job and not voluntary.

How to organize

The question of how to organize this massive effort is on everyone's mind. The volunteering, working for free, taking own efforts to motivate for a cause, are not the way to do it. This requires a professional approach. People need jobs more than anything else first. The people who are motivated, who have capabilities to organize and have the enthusiasm and find satisfaction in doing this job, should be the one who would do it as a profession. It means, it should be their full-time job and should do it with dedication and sense of responsibility to the organization. The members of the organization should pay their dues to make sure that no other external influence is affecting the work which needs to be done. The corporate sponsors, advertisers and others who contribute to the causes have ulterior motives and will have a different agenda than the one the organization is created with. So, it is important that our organizations should be free of any encumbrances and have only one goal: to serve the interest of the members.

Creating the organizations, motivating people to join, creating the objectives and goals, getting the consensus are not easy and should not be done going back to the drawing board and trying to find ways. The best way is to adopt the systems and practices which already exist and use them. The Everything-People-organization will provide on the website all the information necessary with documents which can be used and adopted without any problem.

3

THE NEW SYSTEM COOPERATIVES

Even though the cooperative movement has been successful in local businesses like food cooperatives, the system change cannot happen with Mickey-Mouse-operations which are inherently inefficient and cannot compete with large multinational corporations. The 21st-century cooperatives will work on the same democratic principles which were part of the previous cooperatives, but they will be technology-enabled, more efficient, cost-effective and scalable businesses. Before we delve into the nitty-gritty of the cooperative business, it is important to know how these private companies around the world became multinational behemoths and what needs to be done in the new system for cooperatives to do well.

Reliance group in India is one of the largest groups of industries. Starting in textiles during the Socialistic-leaning years of India, they have grown into a multi-billion-dollar multinational corporation. A few years back the two Ambani brothers Mukesh and Anil Ambani, put up a charade of separating from each other and divided the empire and walked away with a few companies each like the children do after a fight: just pick up whatever toys they can get. But, the only difference from the toys was that the companies each got now are quadrupled in value and the fight turned out to be a master-stroke. Their empire now has companies in almost every industry or sector, telecommunication, infrastructure, Oil & gas, energy, textile, retail, jewellery and even in chappals. What is the secret of their success, are they the genius whiz kids who know everything and master of all trades? No way, they are the rich kids who got the empire handed over to them from their father and with right connections to the government. With all the help from crony capitalism at its best, they could make money. The GDP-growth-obsessed state and central governments are bending over backwards to give huge subsidies in terms of land and tax-breaks to these companies if they decide to set up a factory or retail store in their state and city.

The expertise required for a rich person to start a business in any sector today is none. A group of rich investors can just take over a car manufacturer (example Chrysler) or even a communication company without knowing anything about the sector. Also, you can be just a marketing company around the world for products you do not manufacture nor own but, just market it with a brand name. Nike is the best example of a company which can create products out of thin air and then make money in every country in the world just by advertisement. The biggest secret of these companies is Info-Tech. Information Technology has accelerated the growth of these companies. The ERP or Enterprise Resource Planning, sales and marketing software or e-commerce software systems allow the companies to manage 10, 1000, 100,000 or a million employees or a billion-dollar company without knowing anything about that business. The Ambanis are not some whizz kids who built the group of industries with their genius but, just opportunists with money left by their father. All the large corporations and groups in India are primarily from the time when they had a monopoly in certain sectors which their sons and daughters continued and expanded when the opportunities opened for the private sector in the 1990s. The oligarchic system which is seen in Russia is replicated successfully in India when the opportunity arises. The oligarchs in India are just a handful of families like Ambanis, Tatas, Birla, Godrej, Bajaj, etc., who own almost every business in every sector.

This trend is also a reflection of the politics in India and around the world. Almost all the oligarch families are into real estate development because the rules are made such that it helps these companies to acquire land at cheap prices. For example, a Tata group has a manufacturing facility in Mumbai with 10 Acres of land. Government asks the industry to move out of the city, promising 100 acres of land outside the city. The industry moves to the new location and overnight become an infrastructure development company for the 10 acres of land within the city and another billion dollars added to the group. If the government is not complacent with these groups, why would they get to retain the property when a much large alternative land is provided outside the city? Anyway, to break this government-industry nexus, it is important that the government elected should have people's welfare as the priority and if the people want industries and are comfortable with giving concessions, only people can decide rather than industries influencing the government.

It is important that we mimic the industries which have been successful around the world in our cooperative structure. The notion of starting the small businesses in cooperative structure will not lead to any progress in the field. For example, a food cooperative started by the local enthusiast cannot compete with a food supermarket chain which has hundreds of stores with an efficient supply chain. To compete, you may have to start the cooperative in a model similar to the supermarket chain with an efficient supply chain and technology. If the supermarket model is not profitable, go directly with an online store and delivery which will employ more people, is cost-effective and reduces food waste. This strategy gives us an upper hand in competing with the supermarkets and building efficient businesses in the cooperative structure. The notion of a few guys joining together to build a cooperative business from scratch is futile and irrelevant today.

The example of oligarchs going into every business sector is the one to study. When they start a company to enter a certain sector, they would first look at how to bulldoze other companies in the same field. They are banking on the name-recognition and deep pockets to capture the markets. But, when a cooperative is established, they neither have name-recognition nor are cash-rich, which is a huge negative, unless a different strategy is adopted which gives us the advantage. The biggest advantage of the cooperative business is its members. The small investors who invest money in the cooperatives have the greatest benefit if they use the products and services provided by the cooperative. A corporation spends millions to advertise to get customers to buy their products and services. The customer-acquisition cost varies from 10 to 50% of the total cost of products and services. The cooperatives have ready customers,—their own members—which is a big advantage and part of the savings can be passed to the members and as shareholders, the profits are shared among them. You cannot think of a more efficient model which also provides jobs and works only for their benefit.

The cooperative cannot work in isolation and will be just one part of the new system which enhances the effectiveness of the cooperatives. Imagine that all the necessary funding for the cooperative is provided by the cooperative bank; there is an efficient BPO and a helpdesk to provide the support; there is the technology required to manage the cooperative and the consumer organizations provide the customers; then, you have an efficient and equitable system.

Based on the different sectors, the new cooperatives are derived from six existing businesses which the large businesses use successfully around the world.

1. Online and Mobile-based Products and Service Providers

2. Ancillary plants in manufacturing

3. White-label model of international brands

4. Large retailers' brand products

5. Franchise-business

6. All local community service businesses

Online and mobile-based product-and-service providers

The product and services which were provided earlier at the local level are being managed online and over a mobile phone. It is important to know that nothing has changed locally; the same taxi drivers are driving people around; the same plumbers, electricians and handymen are doing the work locally; the same hospitals are providing the services, but all these services are 'managed' using online and mobile software tools. The Uber has little value-addition to a taxi running in the city except that the booking is done using a mobile app. The notion of this trend is innovative is ridiculous and the taxi booking app charging 25% of the revenue is outrageous. The only reason Uber could expand in so many countries and cities is the power of Info-Tech and the business-model is so fragile that a person with a laptop and the programming tools can develop this app in few weeks. The examples of these so-called innovative models are numerous. Apps which provides the service to facilitate payments in one place, an app which books the tickets for concerts, movies and sports event, apartments, air tickets and hotels, etc., are having billions of dollar valuations. How do we do it efficiently and in a cooperative way? Consider the example of Uber replacement for a city.

A taxi-provider and shared-ride-providers create a cooperative. The cooperative will work for the benefit of the drivers and other service providers. The taxi cooperative licences the app to manage the booking, provide routes, integrate payment interface and help the customers to manage their rides. The licence cost, the device cost and technology management cost to the cooperative will be about 5%. The taxi cooperative subcontracts the support services to the help desk cooperative with a cost of 5%. The rest of the ride billing (90%) is for the drivers, management of cooperative and the cooperative shareholders who are drivers themselves. The management of cooperative will make sure that the best practices are put in place, the drivers and other service providers are given proper training and skills required to provide excellent service. The service depends on the drivers in any model whether it is Uber or a cooperative and in a cooperative, the drivers will be more receptive to providing good service as they are the drivers as well as owners of the business.

When Uber decided to test the self-driving cars, it drove the last nail in its coffin. The greed of not being satisfied with the exorbitant 25% to 30% commission and trying to corner the entire ride revenue by eliminating the drivers is death-nail to the company. I am sure people are excited about seeing a car driving itself but, when it eliminates thousands of jobs, there is no way that they will accept it. But, this flawed business-model will not see the light of the day as the cooperatives would have driven Uber out of business before it is ready to implement it.

Cooperative system is the future of successful business and by using the technology tools, any business can be converted into a successful cooperative business. The list of online and mobile-based businesses which can be converted is endless and the subsequent chapters describe how it can be implemented in detail. Some of the businesses are listed below:

♦ Taxi and rideshare

♦ Travel and Transport Air, train, bus and hotel, movers and packers booking

♦ Event, movies, shows and other bookings

♦ Apartment, homestay and shared housing

♦ Local services handyman, plumbing, electricians, etc.

Ancillary plants in manufacturing

Many of us do not remember the ancillary plants of the industrial era. An ancillary plant is a small plant supplying spare parts for larger unit manufacturing products like automobiles, etc. In most cases, they do not have a marketing department and any other overheads. The unit is small, but they have the same technology and automation as the large manufacturing unit because the large companies share it with them to make them 100% quality-certified. These were essential units of the manufacturing plants but, independent companies run by small entrepreneurs. As mentioned, in most cases, they are 100% quality-certified to supply to the large companies to avoid defects and inspections.

In order keep the cost of parts low and making the parts coming out of these small units to be 100% certified, the large company works with them to streamline the process, help them procure technology and automation required as well as guide them to use the best practices. This worked very well for everybody involved where the large company need not have to hire and fire people, they did not have to build the plants for spare parts and the small businesses do not need to have overheads, marketing and fluctuating demand and enjoyed a steady income.

Large retailer brand products

Many of the retail giants like Walmart, Costco, Target, etc., use this model to fill their shelves with their own brand by using ancillary plants to manufacture products with their brand name. Again, this works well for small manufacturing or food processors to cut costs and be efficient by not having marketing and advertisement expenses and many overheads. You can see hundreds of thousands of products on the shelves with the retailer brands much cheaper than the international brands.

The model shows that many things can be manufactured or processed locally with the highest quality. The milk products are examples in India which are cooperative, but, they did not use the successful model (Amul) to replicate in every state in India. The cooperative model for any industry or product should be such that it can be replicated everywhere. The local brands can either manufacture in their own name or in the name of the retailers.

White-Label products

A **White-Label** product is produced by one company and the other marketing companies rebrand these products in their own names. This is basically, creating products from thin air and buying products cheaper and rebrand and sell it at a much higher price with their own name. The same product in many cases is rebranded by many companies which sell it. The only differentiating factor is the better advertising campaign and who can shout louder on TV and radio ads.

Basically, the rebranding companies do not add any value but, consumers end up paying more for the same product. This is prevalent in electronics, computers, garments and even in automobiles. How can the cooperatives use this model? Well, as the definition of White-Label suggests, the cooperative can be put together and create a brand for necessary items and sell it at a much cheaper price than the other brands.

Franchise-business

The fast-food restaurants started the trend of franchising and it is the most successful business-model available around the world. Even though the small entrepreneurs run the business, it is vulnerable to job retrenchment. The franchisees pay a hefty franchise fee and struggle to recover it through business. This model is more efficient due to

1. The purchasing power of large corporations

2. Stable quality with researched products

3. Efficient due to technology as well as the design of the infrastructure.

4. Brand identification

The service industry

The service industry spans across several sectors and in most cases, it is considered that the smaller local companies and businesses are inefficient and large and multinational companies are efficient and cheaper. However, efficient use of IT tools, internet and mobile converts every small group, small business, cooperative and self-help groups into an efficient workforce.

The gig-economy workers, working in Ola, Uber, Swiggy, etc., are examples of the individual workers being efficient with the use of technology. The Ola cab can be ordered anytime anywhere and the cab will be there at the exact time the app says it will reach. The cab will take you to your destination at the shortest time in the least congested route. But, as they are gig-economy workers without any benefits most of the money collected goes to the app aggregator (25 to 30%), car EMI payment, repairs, insurance and fuel.

Many of these drivers are uneducated and come from small towns. When this can be achieved with technology, think of how efficient the service will be if the drivers are well-paid and well-trained. The service industry is always local, and it employs most of the workforce in the cities around the world. This industry spans from transportation, healthcare, education, delivery, housekeeping, security, real estate, travel booking and many more sectors which need to be removed from the clutches of the large corporations and made it into true local business by providing the necessary technology at low cost.

The new economic System

The capitalists and socialists had a system for each sector from manufacturing to services. The system is how the corporations operate: either completely private or government-owned. Both systems are obsolete and there is a middle-ground with businesses owned by people. For example, the banking sector has a system of debits, credits and interest. Over the period, the methods of deposits, withdrawal and transactions have changed, but the system remains the same. The banks have customers who deposit money, withdraw money, take loans, etc., the system being the same; the banking has evolved from paper ledgers and passbooks to online and mobile banking—the most advanced banking software which provides different ways to transact, mimic the paper ledger system. The banks also have investors who invest the money to enable the bank to start and grow. The software technology-enabled banks to service millions of customers with fewer and fewer employees increasing the profit of the investors multiple times. The customers are doing everything (deposits, withdrawal through ATM, online and mobile) and the banks do not need any employees at all. The physical bank locations which can house about 50 employees are managed by 2 or 3 people. The phone-customer-support can be totally automated with Artificial Intelligence of modern computer systems. This is a typical example of a jobless growth of the business and country where employees are redundant.

The banking is also a perfect example where the investor (capitalist) is not required with cooperative banking. The cooperative banking would have small local investors who would also be employees or customers of the bank. Using the same technology system (ATM, mobile and online software interface) all the services can be provided. Even though this will not increase employment, it will redistribute the profits among the people and reduce the flow of income to the top. Also, with the cooperative having a 1:6 or 1:8 ratio of salaries for the upper management, it will increase the profit to the small local shareholders. The notion that the cost of technology required to match the big banks is very high is not true and it is affordable for even cooperatives. In fact, Information Technology has created a level playing field for big or small banks. So, there is no advantage for the big banks and cooperative banking can have the same advantage.

There is one more major advantage for cooperative banks which the big banks do not have, i.e., ready customers. When the investors and the customers are the same, as in the case of cooperatives, the cost of acquiring customers is zero. The big banks must advertise and spend a huge amount for marketing which can be saved and shared by the cooperative stakeholders (employees, investors and the customers). The new economic system's major card is this model where all the stakeholders are the beneficiaries of the technology and efficiency gains.

The new system can be applied to most of the businesses and industries where the capitalists are artificially creating their importance and cornering all the profits. In sectors like manufacturing, where the capital requirement is high, the state and cooperative banks can act as investors and keep the profits within the stakeholders by using the same automation and technology to create quality products.

For the service sector, including the sales and marketing of the products, the local self-help groups or mutual-aid groups of 10 to 20 members each for different types of services are being trained sporadically all over the world. These need to be made into a must-have in every area, town, and city throughout the country.

Local-area self-help groups

The local-area self-help groups or mutual-aid groups are mostly a group of local service providers for different purposes. They would be individuals who are providing all types of services required for the residents of the local area, town, or city. The individuals need to be grouped together based on their skills and type of job or service they provide and possibly brought under a cooperative or a federation.

In India, the self-help groups for both rural and urban areas are set up in many cities and rural villages. A group of ten poor women join together and form a self-help group and the banks provide small revolving loans to these groups to conduct some micro business. However, due to the lack of technical support and expertise, the business is hardly successful, and they end up with debt on their backs. The system is designed very well and suitable for the new economic system if the groups are provided with technology to manage, a market for their products or services provided and other support.

4

SUPPORT SYSTEM FOR THE PEOPLE

The modern-day corporations have evolved into lean and mean operators. They do not want to do anything which is not their core competence, or which are not profit centres. The rest of the things which are expense centres, or which do not directly add value would be outsourced. The prime example of it is the technology requirements, HR, payroll, sales, marketing and in most cases manufacturing. We must wonder what is left. Nike, which has so many products in sports equipment and sportswear, is a design and marketing company. They do not manufacture anything. Then, how did they become so big? It is purely through marketing and branding. My friend who is a brand manager for a mobile phone company told me the breakdown of the cost of a mobile phone. A phone which sells for 150 USD costs only 50 USD to procure (not manufacture, it will be less than that) from China. They keep $15 for warranty and maintenance (this does not mean they spend it, it only means they keep it aside $15 and then they save more than half from it). The branding with a celebrity brand ambassador and advertisement would cost another $15. A $25 would go to the dealers and distributors. Remaining $55 would be their profits among the management and shareholders. So, basically, about $8 to $10 goes to the end-people in the sales team. This is the type of percentage of profits for most of the products which squander the income of people influenced by the advertisement. The companies which are just doing marketing using somebody else's products are just support-companies and not really business as such. A better marketer can emerge and dismantle them in a second as there is nothing original about their products and services. It also means that anyone can start this kind of company and profit from it by using predatory advertisements or any other means to do business; all they need is money. The stupid rich investors are just swayed by huge profits invested in these companies for short-term gains.

The example I gave where a company procures the products cheaply, get some IT company to build the online marketplace, have a BPO and support company to do all the order processing and deploy distribution and delivery company to deliver, is how most of the online businesses work in real life. This is true for all the marketing and online products and services-based companies which form about 70% of present-day companies. So, when these companies can be started by anyone with money, can we do it with little money and in a cooperative way? Yes, we can do it if only we have all the technology and support we need to make it successful. The BPO and support services of the new system are one piece of the puzzle which is the new system.

The BPO (Business Process outsourcing) and Support Services are required for all the businesses, more so for marketing the companies and mostly outsourced to low-wage countries to make more profits. If the same BPO and support services are provided by local workers, the companies' profits are reduced, but when the cooperatives work for the betterment of the workers and local populations, the question of high profits does not arise. The cooperatives in various sectors can utilize the BPO and support services from the local cooperative BPO and support services and still be efficient and low-cost. Yes, the BPO and support services are offered by a cooperative like the IT workers' cooperatives and support all the cooperative businesses in all the sectors.

A few years back, the BPO and support services required a huge investment in technology. The new cloud technology has changed all that. You can have a Support call-centre operational in a week with little or no investment, just monthly fee for cloud-hosted CRM and dialling and call-receiving application. This also has given the opportunity for people to work from home further reducing the cost of infrastructure. With this technology and reduction in cost, you would think that the companies would hire local people to do tasks which do not deal with secure data, but they do not. They are finding more ways to reduce cost by using Artificial Intelligence to eliminate even those workers in low-wage countries. This cycle of greed will never end and will ultimately lead to complete joblessness and chaos. This trend needs to be reversed by demanding our piece of the pie through a concerted effort of developing a new system which has an equitable outcome for everyone.

As I mentioned, BPO & Support Services provided locally is the key to the new system along with technology and local service centres. The local service centres will host the BPO & call-centre for the local people to access. The BPO and Support Service cooperative employee will work on various projects like HR, Payroll, distribution, delivery, product procurement, ticketing, appointment booking, and many other services required for the local people. Based on the type of work, the employees would have the opportunity to work part-time, full-time, from the service centre or from home. But the important thing is that if these support services are about 10 to 15% of the total economic activity of the country, these cooperatives will make the 10 to 15% of the total GDP. If the technology will make it easy for them to do their job, let the employees enjoy the benefits rather than the corporate shareholders or the rich.

The process of moving back the customer service and BPO jobs to the local areas requires the local people to recognize the importance of having jobs in local cities and towns. I am not saying they do not, but they are not doing anything about it. As the first step in the new system, there should be an organization of the residents. The residents will then elect the local government which represents them and make laws which are beneficial to them and not to corporates. The representatives will make sure that all the outsourcing of customer service and back-office processing should be given to the cooperative which handles these issues with the local workforce. Well, it does not start with the government giving work to the local cooperative but, it starts with the formation of the local government, state government and federal government. It is in the hands of the resident associations which, based on their needs and requirements, elect the right government representatives among themselves to represent them. Also, the government cannot give the work outside of the local people-jobs, which can be done by the local people. This job as a BPO and customer services person is a basic skill which can be acquired through training and can be performed without any problem.

The idea of volunteers used by the government representatives is the biggest scam perpetrated by politicians and corporates. When you can spend millions of dollars on advertisement and other unnecessary activities, can't you pay the persons who are doing the groundwork? People need jobs and what better way than providing jobs to people in the local community? The local BPO and customer service centre cooperative should be given the paid job of doing the groundwork for any campaign.

The products and services provided by large corporations require customer-support and in most cases, it is outsourced and located in other countries. But, despite this blatant lack of concern for the people and consumers, the people still buy the stuff from these companies and proudly display them. It is time we make these companies accountable and get the piece of the pie we deserve. The location of customer care centres in local areas will be a good start.

No matter what the business-model of these companies is, unless consumers realize and recognize what is important for them, there will not be any change. For this, it is important to create organizations of people who will work for them and make decisions together which will be in only our interest. Also, the business models of most of the companies are very fragile and it can be emulated and companies built in the cooperative way. The BPO and support services which are common services for every industry and sector will expedite the process and help in reversing the trend from the rich getting richer and everyone will have equitable employment and income.

5

INFORMATION TECHNOLOGY TOOLS

The Information Technology sector is the backbone of the modern economy. It started as the tool which will complement the work people do rather than replace them. When the bank customers increased, say, from 1000 to a million, it was not possible to do the banking in paper ledgers and other manual means even if the manpower was increased as per the increase in customers. Human errors would be too big to sustain. These software programmes automated the existing process and helped the bank employees to do their work efficiently. Information Technology tools were rapidly deployed in all the sectors and helped every sector from healthcare, education, manufacturing, logistics, etc. to become efficient. With this requirement of Information tools in all sectors, a whole new industry was developed which generated a large number of highly skilled employees and the people with analytical abilities and a degree in science, maths or engineering got opportunities to design and develop these software tools. These tools over a period, proved to be the death-nail for the employees of all sectors as the automation and technology required fewer and fewer employees. This is due to the capitalist nature of the companies whose only goal is to make money and if the Information Technology tools reduced the work of the employees, the employees became the liability and it would be against the goal of the company to retain them. This is seen in the rapid job losses in every sector and inequality due to the benefits of this technology and reduction in manpower going straight to the investors.

The software technology itself has come a long way from the initial development tools used. The software tools improved and many tasks and programmes were automated to make it efficient and can be replicated without any developers and programmers being required. A programme once developed can be customized with minor changes for many applications rather than developing a whole new application. The IT industry which was growing rapidly employing a huge number of highly skilled employees throughout the 1990s and 2000s is now in decline. The survey finds that in next five years, the employee-strength in IT industry will be half of what it is today, but the IT industry itself is growing rapidly with Artificial Intelligence, and machine learning tools are developed which can be deployed in healthcare, education, manufacturing, etc. This decline in manpower and increase in the profits are again going to the company management and investors which will create more inequality and job losses.

The impact of the Information Technology tools on different industries can be seen in the rapid growth of another allied industry which is IT-Enabled Services (or ITES). It is simply services offered using the IT tools. For example, the travel industry depended on travel agents around the world to book their hotels, train tickets and flight tickets. This small-scale industry employed a healthy number of people in the industry based on revenue. But the online travel booking sites and tools made it possible for the customers themselves to book their tickets without the help of the travel agents. The *Expedia, MakeMyTrip, Clear Trip, Trivago*, etc., have eliminated the job of local travel agents. The travel industry itself grew to a large extent but, the number of employees declined rapidly. The service providers (like airlines, hotels, etc.) themselves are reducing the manpower by automating many of the tasks which the employees did. The automated check-in, baggage-handling, etc. have proved job killers and the profit goes to the top management and the investors. The ITES industry is required for the scale, but it should be to ease the work of the services industry workforce rather than replacing them.

The combination of IT & ITES may be the single largest reason for the decline in employment and income-inequality. There are many ITES companies with billions of dollars in valuation and revenue with very few employees compared to the size. The startup companies are mostly in the ITES sector where people are discovering various ways to automate the physical process and make money. It is seen in finance, real estate, healthcare, education, etc., and the trend is dangerous for every national government as they must deal with a generation of unemployed youth. The misconception of the new-age start-ups providing the nation with rapid growth is there for everyone to see. There is growth, but it is a jobless growth for which the major culprit is the IT & ITES industry. This does not mean that we go back to the Stone Age and do everything manually, but find ways where the benefit of this IT efficiency and automation goes to many, not a few. The trend by the companies to reduce manpower and profit from it as soon as some automation tool is available to replace them should stop and the companies should be morally and socially responsible towards the communities and employees and should share the profits with the employees; but, since the structures of these companies are not created to be morally and socially responsible, it is time to change the structure of the companies to make sure they are morally and socially responsible. To do that, we must go towards democratic cooperative companies. Since the IT & ITES form the core of efficiency needs of all other sectors and industries, the IT & ITES should be the core cooperatives which must be there in every nation to protect the employees and be the first one to be created in the new economic system.

The Information Technology tools ranging from desktop software, online portals, mobile apps and Artificial Intelligence are most essential for the new system; however, the benefit of making and using these tools should go to the workers/investors and the customers. Since the workers themselves are the investors and shareholders, if they lose their job due to automation, they get the income as investors and shareholders of the cooperatives. This is not the way the industry operates at present. A billion-dollar company can be started and operated from a garage, a free open-source software built by a group of enthusiasts can run half of all the internet servers in the world; it is time to think how the IT sector can be tamed, managed and run. It is important to stop and think about the stakeholders in the sector, who should benefit and how much to benefit.

In the late 1990s when the Info-Tech was exploding, the capitalists were too eager to get the first-mover advantage in all the Info-Tech companies without knowing anything about it. The *.com* bubble was the biggest example of insane market capitalization of *.com* companies which had nothing to show. A company with 30 employees with a business-model to build an online marketplace had a market capitalization of $35 billion. About a billion dollars for every employee. The online marketplace was literally the replica of the products' brokerage firms which were for years matching the buyers and sellers physically. Anyway, the collapse was inevitable, and I see that capitalists are still fascinated with Info-Tech in all its new avatars, social networks, big data, cloud computing, Artificial Intelligence without knowing the scam of new wine in an old bottle. Having been in the IT industry for over 20 years and building systems, I have always thought that it is a scam. Well, let me explain. Back in 1996, I was part of a project to build a comprehensive project management system for all the US State department of transportations. The project took two years to build at a cost of $20 Million. For the next 10 years, around $50 million was spent to maintain and upgrade the system, not because of the changes to the business rules or new requirement, but mostly due to the operating system upgrade and the developmental tool upgrade. There was absolutely no value-addition, but huge money was spent on it. Not all projects are like this, but I would say, 60 to 70% of the project upgrades and technology conversion projects are waste and scam.

It may be argued that well, the programmers and developers had jobs because of this, but it is not the case here. Most of the money in IT also goes to the top to the management and corporates. Out of every dollar spent on the IT project, only about 20 to 25% goes to the people doing the work and 75 to 80% goes to the overheads. It is high time, the IT&ITES sector is overhauled and real value-added work is done, and the IT workers are paid their due.

The IT products and services have created this situation where a large number of the non-IT workforce can be eliminated without any consequence for a corporation. Prior to this, to eliminate the workforce, the corporations had to go to great lengths of moving the entire manufacturing to low-wage countries. Now, you just have to bring in a few programmers and build a system which does everything right in the country or best of all, outsource it to some offshore company in India and you need only a few people to run your entire global organization.

Take the banking and finance sector in the US, which is 30% of the GDP and employs only 5% of the employees. The sector is growing, and employees are being reduced and the profit from this reduction in employees is going straight to the top management and shareholders. This is the first sector which needs to be fully cooperative to make sure that 30% of the income goes to at least 30 % of the people. The discrepancy in employment in this sector is mostly due to the technology in the way of ATMs, online and mobile banking, automated stock trading, etc.; with the cooperative model, the profits would go to people instead of large bank shareholders. The lure of big banks is only in the fact that they are international. When people travel around the world, they need to bank somewhere. But, with the technology available for banking from anywhere and anytime, the small cooperative bank can become an international bank. So, there is absolutely no need for banking in big banks. People need to understand how the big banks use our money to gamble and know that if their bet wins, the banks win and if the bet is lost, we lose. This mismatch is in every sector of the economy and the employees are rapidly disappearing.

The IT industry itself has a huge mismatch when compared to the % of GDP to the employees. The top IT-related companies' founders' net worth is about a trillion dollars. It is also a misconception that the founders are geniuses and they deserve the wealth they have accumulated. They completely depend on the employees with expertise and tools developed by open-source software to enrich themselves. When the IT is used in the new system with cooperatives, this trend will completely stop and there will be equitable distribution of income among all the people who are involved in the IT industry. There are many software tools available, which can be developed or customized to use them in the new system to benefit everyone.

The open-source software is the software developed by likeminded IT enthusiasts all over the world. It is available for anyone to use it for free. The statistics are mind-boggling. Half of the internet web pages use the open-source web server. A huge percentage of databases runs on the open-source database management system. The content management systems are all open-source. Most of the large corporations use these tools to profit from it, but the people who developed this open-source software do not get paid. This system must change and the people who spend their time and expertise to build these systems need to be paid their dues and this must be brought under a cooperative system to make it equitable and just for everyone. Yes, the IT workforce will work well in a cooperative environment and they will form the driving force for all other democratic cooperative businesses to make them efficient and low-cost to provide income from the savings to people and make it an equitable economy

Cooperative for the IT workforce

The cooperative model for the IT workforce is most essential to make sure most of the income goes to the workers rather than to top management and rich investors. The cooperative model does not mean everyone is paid the same salary, but equitable salary based on skill and experience. Since the shareholders in the cooperatives are the IT-related workers, the income is shared by everyone. When the software is developed, and extremely limited work is required, the income from the sale of software to the cooperatives will provide the income to the workers. Many IT workers who work as independent contractors or consultants can be part of the cooperative to benefit from the healthcare and retirement benefits from it. Also, when the software and AI automate all the work and very few IT workers are required, but still generating the same amount of profits and income, these profits and income will go to the shareholders of the cooperative rather than to the investors of the large companies.

The IT consulting business is a multi-billion-dollar industry with all the big names like IBM, Accenture, TCS, Infosys, etc., dominating the landscape. It is nothing but a head-hunting operation with the qualified engineers and technologists doing all the work while the companies take 30 to 40% profit. There are hundreds of small players who try to penetrate the market at secondary and tertiary level, but end up with crumps and pay their employees peanuts while the chain of consulting companies makes the most profits. In between this insane system, the banks make huge profits extending overdraft facilities to every level of companies to pay their contractors or sub-contractors while waiting for the 90-days-to-6-months' payment cycle the end-project companies follow. Meanwhile, the IT contractors and consultants go from project to project in different cities and countries working long hours in a stressful work environment. These consulting companies which do not add any value should be replaced by the cooperative which deals directly with the end-client with the consultants working in the cooperative and the cooperative shareholders support the payment cycle while reducing the cost to the client and sharing most of the profits by the consultant and the cooperative shareholders. The cooperative also provides the varied skill-set required by different industries and provide the right advice and suggestion without bias to the clients.

The IT cooperative will put an end to this exploitation and stress. There is no need for the IT cooperatives to make 30 to 40% profits; only 10 to 15% would be a good profit and the rest of it should go to the worker. The profit after the expenses of the cooperative will go again to the workers themselves. This will be the biggest competitive advantage of the cooperative which can outbid every large IT project. The corporates, businesses and government will start directly working with the cooperatives owned by the IT workforce to reduce the cost and get the required software for a reasonable price. This also will be the way to move the billions from the top management to the workers.

The 'bench' time in IT vocabulary means that the consultant has no assignment and working in-house. Despite being in the IT industry, I have never been on 'bench', but I always imagined people sitting in line on the physical bench. It is also the time the companies use their employees to develop some products which they can sell or provide the employees time to get more skill training. As a cooperative owned by IT workers, they can utilize this time to contribute to their own software to build a vast array of software required which are priced expensive by the IT companies. This ownership gives the employees a chance to contribute to their own future earnings during their downtime as well as in retirement. If the trend of automation continues, it is predicted that half the IT workforce will be out of work, but if they own these automation tools, they can simply enjoy the downtime.

The IT cooperative will work as a collective for all the IT workers as well as provide the necessary support to all the other industries. The objectives, products and services are:

Objectives

♦ To provide the IT workers with a platform to own and manage their own democratic organization which will give them the satisfaction of work, a good income and share their expertise to the betterment of the people

♦ To acquire, lease or develop, customize and manage software products and application to make them available to other industries, people and government at a reasonable cost

♦ To provide skill-enhancement, training and mentoring for IT professionals in different skills to provide them with employment and entrepreneurial opportunities

♦ To provide IT recruitment, consulting and contracting services to different industries and government with the right workforce for their needs

♦ To host and manage software as a service for members and customers for providing the software at a reasonable price

♦ To partner with small and medium IT & ITES companies to market, support their products and services to give them a bigger platform to sell their products, provide their services and support their services

Products and services

1. Using mostly open-source software, develop products and applications for other industries, cooperatives and government

2. Manage Software as a service

3. IT recruitment

4. IT consulting and contracting

5. IT-skills development

6. Training and career development

7. Cloud hosting ownership and management

8. Customer-support services

Power of People cooperatives

The billion-dollar IT consulting companies in the US and India are running only on the back of the highly skilled employees and when there is a downturn, all the employees are disposable. The consulting companies which make a profit of more than 30% to 50% have little value-addition and are happy having contract employees passing through them and making huge profits. When people are the assets and knowledge-base for these companies, do we need them to enslave us and make money out of us? These IT & ITES workforce cooperatives will work towards making the workers the key to software development, consulting and other activities. Also, when the entire economy now depends on the IT systems, tools and services, IT workers who are the knowledge-workers for the economy should be the ones who should manage, drive and profit from this revolution. If used as collective and cooperative means, the sector which created this mess of income-inequality is the one which will reverse the trend and make it equitable for people

How is a cooperative different from a company?

The IT & ITES works differently compared to a corporate in several different ways:

1. The shareholders are the people who are related to the IT industry

2. Every shareholder has one vote rather than one vote for every share owned

3. CEO and management can make only eight times the average salary compared to corporate CEO's making 300 or 400 times more than the average employee

4. If the IT workers lose their job, they still get revenue from the shareholding

5. If the IT worker or team who developed software and the software is deployed or sold by the cooperative, the revenue from this software sale or service provided will go to the team and the shareholders

6. Collaboration advantage with knowledge-sharing rather than competition

7. Huge reduction in overhead expenses and management salaries

Collaboration advantage

Collaboration among software development teams across the world is possible seamlessly. There may be several teams and individuals working together across the world on one project. Many IT professionals work from home and from many remote locations. The technology and software tools provide that infrastructure to collaborate from anywhere. This is the biggest advantage of the software development environment which suits very well for collaborative work. When we consider IT cooperative, the overhead expenses can be reduced drastically using these collaborative infrastructures without moving people around unnecessarily adding to the expenses for getting software developed, maintained and upgraded without physical movement of people.

This collaboration among remote teams works very well in a cooperative environment. The corporates are least bothered about spending money of the client in travel and other expenses. Travelling to different places for projects may sound fancy for some people; it becomes a health risk for many. It also unnecessarily takes time out of family time.

The process

♦ Anyone aged 18 years or older who is studying or training to work or working in IT & ITES or related fields can become a member of the EP Technologies cooperative society.

♦ Only members can become shareholders, shareholders-and-consultants, contractors or employees depending on the need of the cooperative and need of the members.

♦ Members can avail the recruitment services through the recruitment portal and career counselling services to be placed in different companies, government and cooperatives as employees.

♦ Members can avail consulting and contracting services to be placed in different companies, government and cooperatives as temporary contractors or consultants.

♦ Members can avail the skill training and counsellor services for job placement as well as for job enhancement.

♦ Members can purchase, systems, software and other requirements through the cooperative at bulk purchase prices.

♦ Members can participate in software development part-time, full-time or as a consultant based on their skill in cooperative projects or partner companies.

♦ Members can bring new project ideas and develop the project in partnership with the cooperative to be marketed, hosted and maintained by the cooperatives on a profit-sharing basis.

♦ Members can avail healthcare services, insurance, banking and financial services and other products and services from the partner cooperatives.

♦ Members can become shareholders in other partner cooperatives to avail related products and services.

The cooperative partnership model

Small and medium IT & ITES related companies with less than 100 employees will be a partner with the technology-cooperative. The partners who are small and medium companies carry huge overheads to market their products and services. Very few of these companies scale to be large multinational companies and most of them struggle to find business, manpower and profitability due to their size. With the partnership with the technology-cooperative with thousands of members, they will get the platform to participate in large projects, develop products and applications. The companies can be in software development, training, system integration, product-and-service providers, recruitment or consulting. The partnership will be based on the objectives of the cooperative and on cost or profit-sharing basis. With thousands of members or shareholders, the technology-cooperative will be able to compete with any large company for projects in government, private and cooperative sector. This partnership will be similar to the ancillary units in manufacturing where the partners can depend on a steady flow of business to their company based on the skills and capabilities available.

Advantages of the partnership model

1. The technology-cooperative with thousands of members and partners will be a huge platform for IT & ITES workforce to have a successful and satisfying career and steady income.

2. Give a platform for hundreds of small and medium companies to succeed and flourish.

3. Reduce the overheads of these companies in recruitments, marketing, purchasing, customer-support, maintenance and management.

4. Mutual availability of skilled manpower, knowledge-base for collaborative growth.

5. Participate in large projects for different industries, government and organizations.

6. Develop software products in cooperative to be used to compete with the other companies to benefit shareholders of cooperatives and partner companies.

Common software and IT systems

The IT cooperative will develop or acquire common software systems which are essential for this cooperative and other related cooperatives in other sectors.

1. Cooperative management system—The cooperative shareholders, employees, contractors, partners, finances and legal compliance are managed using a comprehensive Information management system. All the necessary tools both online and mobile should be available to the cooperative management

to manage with transparency. The shareholders will get the necessary information about the progress of the cooperative, about their dividends, voting requirements, etc. and will be able to give and receive feedback, complaints, concerns as well as suggestions and advice. This management system is the most essential software system for the new economy cooperative.

2. Finance, banking and insurance—The finance, banking and insurance management system is a common software system for any industry-specific cooperative. The payment gateway, mobile wallet, finance management and insurance management software systems are developed or acquired by the technology-cooperative and services provided by the common finance, banking and insurance cooperative.

3. Training and tutoring portal—the online platform for training, tutoring and counselling for any or all the people in the new economic system organizations, cooperatives and other partners and collectives. The platform will be training, counselling and tutoring managed by different cooperatives. The technology-cooperative will acquire, manage and maintain the platform for all other cooperatives.

4. Healthcare Platform—The healthcare management requirement is for everyone and the healthcare online platform to facilitate healthcare services from private or government needs to be streamlined. The telemedicine platform for consultation and other services to reach everyone and Information and network platform to access the right healthcare will be the objective of this network. The technology-cooperative will acquire, manage and maintain the platform for all the other cooperatives, but the healthcare cooperative will manage the service through it.

5. E-commerce platform— the e-commerce platform is required to facilitate the right products and service for members of the cooperatives as well as the network and organization members. The platform will be developed using all the necessary features

used by the e-commerce companies and made available to all the cooperatives. The technology-cooperative will acquire or develop, manage and maintain the platform. The e-commerce platforms are available as open-source and only small customization is required to use it for the cooperative.

6

LOCAL COMMUNITY SERVICE CENTRES

Imagine an online store where you can get everything cheaper than at local stores or supermarkets. Everything delivered right at your doorstep by a robot or drone. All your banking and financial transactions done online or mobile. You can learn online, book tickets online and you can talk to your doctor online. Well, you do not need to imagine as everything I said is already here. Also, another major impact on our lives due to technological change is social interactions. We are now confined to our homes and interact online on social networks with somebody thousands of miles away instead of our local friends and family. But, again, we want the positive changes where our lives are simplified; we can interact with everyone around the world but, also keep the local communities intact.

In terms of the social collective platform, the commercially based online platforms like Google, Facebook, etc., have moved people to their homes and glued to their digital media. I remember a few years back, in one Florida university, John Kerry was speaking, and one student was vocal in asking questions and disrupting the speech. The police were called, and he was tazed and carried out of the auditorium all the while shouting and saying the now-famous words "Don't taze me, bro." There were, maybe, a thousand people in the auditorium and none of them would get up and protest against these brutal police actions; however, the Facebook and other social media flared up and people from the auditorium were posting to protest the action. This is a clear example of the people's inability to interact physically and losing the ability to confront the problems and becoming extreme individuals physically, but collective when they cannot see each other. This phenomenon is not an aberration or an accident, but a systematic influence of capitalism to extract profit from everything. This is seen everywhere with the park benches made as uncomfortable as possible, having no place to sit in supermarkets and other commercial places; the local social centres will address just that. The local social centres are service centres with the intention of service in all respects.

On the outset, it may seem that automation and technology are helping people simplify their life. It is doing it to some extent. If products are purchased online, you get it cheaper and don't have to go to the store; if banking is automated, you can bank from anywhere, but what happens to the people who are working in retail stores or in banks and other local organizations? Of course, they lose their jobs and local revenue. The taxes which are generated by the local activities which support all the local services are in jeopardy due to these technological changes. I used the word technological changes instead of technological innovation, because, it is not innovation. There was a system of doing things locally and physically and now, it is transferred online and in no way it is innovation.

The benefits of these changes directly go to the shareholders of the online companies, banks and technology companies and the losers are the local employees, local people and local government. But, the new system will not suggest going back to the old ways of doing things, but make sure that most of the benefits of these technological changes are shared by the local people.

As social beings, we need interaction; we need space for collective social activities as well as we need access to services locally to keep the government and private products and service providers accountable. Also, when local people in a town, city or village consume products and services, the local people should be benefitted with jobs or source of income. The local commercial entities are not the answer as the cost of doing business locally is not cost-effective anymore. So, the answer is a hybrid system using technology, but the benefit should go to the local people. This can be achieved by having local social centres in every village, town and all areas of the city.

The local social centres are essentially public places for both social interactions as well as for accessing services. These centres should be owned or subsidized by the government like any other infrastructure like roads or bridges, which will remove the pressure of paying rent or paying off the mortgage by the local service providers. The maintenance of the place and amenities should be done by the membership of local people with small fees. The centre will be a social place for interaction without restrictions of obligations of any kind. The types of services which can be accessed through these centres are many. Most of the services do not require a separate building or store and can be housed in a common place. Based on the space and population, the centres can be built large or small and a number of services which can be accessed. But, every village, town and city should have it and they are as essential as parks and recreation centres accessible to the public.

The services which can be accessed from these centres are:

- Park & Ride
- Food and other local deliveries
- Post box and possible post offices
- Cooperative bank branch
- Ticket booking and theatres
- Online-education classrooms
- Agencies for finance, insurance and other products and services
- Telemedicine centre
- Business-centre
- Childcare centre
- Financial and Insurance Services
- Utilities

- Social Services
- Geriatric-care
- Coffee shop
- Laundry collection centre
- Transport and travel services
- Call-centre and BPO

These services which are currently in commercial establishments have too many overheads which make them expensive to people. The rent, financial management, utilities, marketing, procurement and delivery—all the overheads eat up the profits. With this model, the workers or employees make the most of the profits. If these services are established under the cooperative model and the local people are all investors in the cooperative, it will be a form of minimum basic income they can generate out of it. The details of some of the different services are given below.

The 'online-only' stores are the most efficient except when it comes to last-mile-connectivity to deliver the products and services. The last-mile-connectivity becomes more expensive than everything else and no wonder Amazon, the biggest online retailer in the world would think of drones and other methods to deliver. But, is it what we want, a cheaper product at the cost of local employment? Not until the new system is in place. The idea of doing everything online and automating the local jobs like cashiers at McDonald's, Walmart, Target, etc., is a symptom of everything going wrong with capitalism. These multinational establishments are saying that the minimum wage increase would result in no-wage. If the delivery services of these consumer products are managed by this local cooperative and from a local service centre, then part of the online profits are shared by local people.

The Ubers and Lyfts of the world have established themselves around the world in a taxi and shared-ride services. It did give a wakeup call to the taxi companies to improve their services as well as technology based on today's needs. If you think about it, the only thing changed between the taxi companies and Uber is the way you hail a taxi. Earlier, it would be through a call to the central taxi support centre; now, it is using an app. It is interesting to note that we have lost the ability to call a taxi if we do not have internet. While the new way of ride-hailing has caught up and people love it, it is important to see how it has impacted the lives of the people who are providing the service, the drivers. First, the commission of Uber is way more than what the taxi driver used to be paid for the same service: hailing by calling a fully manned call-centre. Also, with these commercial services having the only goal of maximizing the profits, they have started experimenting with self-driving cars to eliminate the pesky drivers. As they say in technical terms, this is a no-go. Any model which eliminates jobs locally and profits the big corporations is not required in the new system.

People seem to like the new way of hailing a cab or to some extent using the shared-ride portion of it; how can we replace it with a model which is local, helpful to people, eco-friendly and helps drivers have decent living? The cooperative is the way to go. The taxi service should evolve by using the same technology as the Uber or Lyft and have comprehensive ridesharing so that it is helpful to people, environment and gives the necessary income to drivers. If the future technology evolves to self-driving cars, the cars will be owned by local cooperatives and the taxi and shared-ride drivers will be shareholders in the cooperative benefit from it. If it means free time for the drivers, and they get the income from the self-driving cars, that is the way the new system will work. The key is to make sure that the single-occupancy vehicles are reduced and the shared rides are increased.

The shared rides can happen if the park-and-ride places are increased and made more accessible to people. The present-day park-and-ride lots are like abandoned parking lots without any type of amenities and not sure the car will be there when they get back. Why can't we make these places more vibrant with amenities like showers, restrooms, coffee shops, childcare centre and shared rides to and from home so that more people can use it? The name is a misnomer as there should be a way for the people who do not have a car also to use it. When it comes to shared rides and public transport, it is not possible to have a direct service from home to office or school or college. It should be such that a last-mile-connectivity-vehicle is provided to the park-and-ride and then a public transport or larger vehicle for the longer ride. This can happen if the last-mile-connectivity providers are housed in park-and-ride-area and available 24/7 for the service. This way, people can be assured that they just need to reach the nearest park-and-ride-place from anywhere and they are assured of the ride to their home. This guaranteed service will assure people not to buy cars or not to use cars for everything.

In addition to the park-and-ride-place providing guaranteed transport service, many services can be added like last-mile-delivery of purchased products online, laundry pickup and drop off, food delivery, etc. These services provided at a reasonable price will help local businesses as well as generate many jobs locally. These park-and-ride-places which are provided now by the local government is a first step in setting up the local social and service centres. The local services which are expensive to manage if a separate store is set up, will work very well if operated from a place where minimal office maintenance fee is charged. In many cities, the park-and-ride-places are already existing which can become a source of employment and easily accessible services.

The shared-ride service providers and most of the service providers in these centres may not have work all the time. So, it is a good place to provide classrooms for online classes so that they can continue their education, training or any other online courses to enhance their skills. It is not advisable to sit at home and take these courses without interacting with the students and peers. These centres offer ready access to the students to get their education online and still interact with other students. The online training and education technology is quite advanced with all the tools available for the students to attend class from teachers, trainers and professors from anywhere.

Many of the marketing and sales jobs allow employees to work from home or from anywhere. Even if this option is available, the employees may not have the infrastructure to support to operate from home. Also, many find it difficult to concentrate at home due to many personal and family reasons. So, these employees end up going to the office unnecessarily adding to the traffic of the city. If there is a park-and-ride centre which may have the business-centre with support staff to assist in infrastructure needs as well as a ready office close to home, it is the best option available. It may also be the place for many self-employed people who want that business-centre-like-support without having to spend a huge amount for an office. These are the kinds of ideas which help the local communities build the required infrastructure for many essential services from these local centres.

The social part is again a very important part of this local infrastructure. It may be required for the local people to meet at a place where they are not obliged to buy stuff or is too far from home. The local centres will act as a place to have get-togethers, parties and other functions which are not accessible to many low-income people. The childcare as part of the centre will provide everyone with access to low-cost support for working parents.

These centres in low-income communities act as a conduit to progress. The people who have no access to many of the essential services will be benefitted enormously. The essential services required for these communities range from childcare, rideshare, public transport, online education and training, telemedicine, business-centre and much more. The decaying cities in the US where gentrification basically displaced low-income families away into further inaccessible areas need this infrastructure to provide the opportunities for employment income which they can earn from working in their neighbourhoods. This also paves the way for them to have access to transport as well as for skills which they cannot access from their homes. If the local government is to promote the opportunities for the low-income and marginalized communities, this would be the first step towards it.

To tilt the balance of power and income from the rich to the rest of us, these centres are essential. It gives the advantage which is lacking in the local businesses to be cost-effective and efficient. Most of the entrepreneurs who want to start their business would do it in the local area and they need the support and additional skills which can be provided by the essential services housed in the centre. However, it is not easy to make the policies by the local, state and federal government to support the new system which obviously will go against the big corporates and the rich; so, the constraints must be overcome at the ballot box during the elections. As they say, democracy is not a spectator-sport and needs the participation of everyone to vote and elect local, state and federal representatives who would take the manifesto prepared by the people and implement it. One of the biggest items in the manifesto should be the social centres for every village, town and city.

As mentioned in the technology section of this book, the technology required for providing efficient services to the local population through the local centre is available in open-source as well as by the technology team of the cooperatives. It is important that this software and technology support is available before the centres are set up. The shared-ride app and management system, online education, training and employment systems, cooperative bank management systems and many other software and management systems should be made available. It would be part of the maintenance and management of the service centres.

7

COLLECTIVE COLLABORATION BETWEEN COOPERATIVES

One of the most important principles of cooperatives is the cooperation between cooperatives. The competition culture of capitalism has pitted one organization against another and in some cases, the cooperatives themselves competing which is against the cooperative principles. It is not a monopoly if the cooperatives are formed by the people who use it and the people who work for it as they correct themselves based on the needs of the people. If there is only one cable company in the region and it is a private one, their goal is to maximize the profits at the expense of the consumers who have no choice available. The private cable company would raise the prices based on the capacity of the population to pay rather than having a business-model of nominal profits over the expenses of providing the service. This would be a monopoly and it is easy for them to have predatory practices to exploit the situation. However, if a cooperative is formed for the same purpose, the investors are local people as well as the workers from the same community. The checks and balances of the investors, consumers and the workers will prevent them from price gouging as well as from providing inferior service.

The private companies have the biggest disadvantage due to the competition. Their customer-acquisition cost is extremely high as they do not have any stake in the community and if they let the guard down, the competition will kill them and take their business. The notion of the prices reducing for the consumers due to the competition is a farce as they simply collude using their industry organizations and keep the prices at a level where the industry makes enough profits to survive and compete using conniving tactics rather than price and customer service. The cooperatives, meanwhile, have a huge stake in the communities and they have both social and business agenda which prevents them from any predatory practices. The consumers, workers and investors of the cooperatives being local and stakeholders, the customer-acquisition cost is zero and that part of the expenses which is huge is shared among all the stakeholders.

A company or cooperative has many requirements to conduct its business of manufacturing or service effectively. The technology is required to manage, automate some of the processes, provide services, communicate with employees, vendors, consumers, receive payments and for paying employees, etc. It requires a support team to support customers and other stakeholders; it needs financial and banking partners, vendors, equipment, workers and many more. Each of these requirements adds to the cost of the product or service provided and large companies can get them at a lower cost than the smaller companies due to size advantage. Irrespective of the business-model, the customers pay for them. If the large company uses their size to their advantage, part of the savings goes to the customers and most of the savings goes to the shareholders and management. However, for a small and local enterprise, the burden of the increased cost due to smaller size has to be absorbed by the company by reducing the profits and the customers pay extra for the same services. The cooperative model will change that. The collaboration between cooperatives will make it efficient and get the same advantage as a large company and the savings are shared by the people rather than large investors and management.

The technology-cooperative will provide all the technology required for the efficient running of any other sector cooperative. The customer service cooperative will provide the support required for all the operations of the specific sector cooperative and the collaboration between the other cooperatives from finance, food, health, education, etc., provide the necessary products and services required. This collaboration is the key to the successful transformation required to move to the people-centric, democratic organization structure. The current cooperatives without the support system are isolated and trying to compete with the large corporations will only depress the enthusiasm people may have for adopting the cooperative model. The collaboration between the cooperatives means that most of the profits from these cooperatives will go to the people instead of the corporates. If the software required for the management of the cooperative is developed or purchased from a software company, they have huge mark-up on the price as well as the scam of customizing the software will cost the cooperative high price. However, the technology-cooperative will use the cooperative members to develop the software using the open-source and reduce both the effort and cost. The technology-cooperative will host, manage and maintain the software at a low cost so that the other cooperatives are free to provide the core services without bothering about the technology.

The other collaborations in managing finance are very important for the success of the cooperative. With the customers and workers as shareholders, it will remove most of the burden as well as a distraction which cripples many small businesses and cooperatives. The additional finances required are provided by the banks, financial and insurance cooperatives. The same applies to all the support services required for the cooperatives to operate efficiently, provide income to workers and provide the best service to the communities. The collective model following the outsourcing perfected by the large corporations is very helpful in the cooperatives; however, it is not to the low-wage countries or other corporations but to other cooperatives which have core competence in that field.

8

WORK AND INCOME IN THE NEW SYSTEM

The total wealth of the US stands at about $71 trillion. This wealth generates about $200,000 per working person per year. The inequality is moving most of the income generated to the top and leaving workers with a pittance. The technology, automation and globalization are the main reasons for this inequality. Every time a new technology is created, workplaces are automated or the manufacturing and other services are moved to other countries, the income starts moving to the top. When the banking sector started using technology to automate the entire banking process, it naturally, eliminated bank tellers and other employees. If the benefits from these changes to the work and jobs were shared with the workers, this extreme inequality could have been avoided, but the corporate structure does not allow this to happen and we end up with this extreme income-inequality. The conventional workers in manufacturing as well as some services were the most affected, but the knowledge-workers (the people who built these systems) did get a boost in their income as their knowledge and skills were required for the transformation. However, their role also is limited as the technology they built can be replicated and deployed without additional input. These knowledge-workers who gave rise to the knowledge-economy also became its victims. The new system has the ways and means to deal with the knowledge-economy and distribute the gains in a more equitable way.

Since the 1990s we have entered a knowledge-economy which means that it is the work which is done using the knowledge acquired during our education, work and other experience. The knowledge can be shared without diminishing it and multiplied without cost. The Information Technology systems can be built using the knowledge and it can be made available to millions without further processing or human intervention. The financial transaction can be done without any intervention from anywhere and everywhere on a computer or a smartphone, thus eliminating hundreds of thousands of banking jobs. In this knowledge-economy, what happens to all the employees who were doing manual jobs or routine jobs? Also, the software professionals who created the system which allows these jobs to be eliminated are no longer required. Once these automated systems are built, it can be propagated without much work required on it. This is the dilemma faced by governments around the world as to how new jobs will be created while the conventional jobs are being eliminated. The answer is to move to the more equitable new economic system.

For long, most of us get our income from the work we do and if we don't have work, we don't earn anything. The other investments and savings are for the time when we retire and most of us live from pay-cheque to pay-cheque. The work-wages have not increased or kept up with inflation, etc., but the cost of living has increased many folds. The consumerization is driving us towards purchasing things beyond our means and the credit is facilitating this habit to an extent that most of us are in huge debt. In addition, automation and technology have reduced the number of jobs while the population is increasing. Since most of us have income from job and wages, the future looks bleak unless we derive a steady income from some other source when we do not have jobs or additional income when we have jobs. The new system cooperatives will be the other income which we will get to tide over when we don't have a job and compensate for the low wages at the job.

The new system cooperatives will be profitable by their structure. Using the same tools and techniques of the corporates but at a lower cost due to collaboration and sharing, the customer-acquisition cost will be low with the community participation and the low executive management salaries. With this structure, the shareholders, the community as well as the workers get the dividends for all the profit the cooperatives make. The idea of the local communities having stake as well as monetary benefit will be a catalyst for the cooperatives to succeed and be profitable. When the automation and technology are used in the cooperatives as may be required, the benefit goes to the workers with additional dividend income which will compensate for the job loss. Also, instead of cutting jobs, the working hours may be reduced to accommodate most of the workers. But the important thing is that the profits remain in the community.

The work or jobs in future in the capitalist system would disappear for sure. Unless we rapidly deploy the cooperative system to replace the corporate entities, the pain will be felt across the nation and the economic condition of most of the workers will deteriorate. There is a lot of talk about universal basic income for all to compensate for the job losses, but the political system is not equipped to make those decisions as the rich hold reigns of the government and will not allow this drain of their income without a fight. If the new system cooperatives are developed properly, they will help significantly to reverse the trend of income and profits going to the rich. In addition, the knowledge-economy is a people-economy and financial capital has limited role and the human capital role is significantly larger. However, the capitalists are still making money in the knowledge-economy exploiting the ignorance of people about the technology and the change it has created. The new system has the structure to highlight the human capital and make sure that the people are benefitted.

The money that is being invested in technology and knowledge-economy is from the financial sector. The financiers realize that the disruptive technologies are cash-low when it can displace a huge number of people from their jobs and that benefit goes to them. But, unlike other industries, the knowledge-workers take their skill and experience to create another company doing the same thing better and cheaper. The same patent rules of other industries do not apply here, and it is easy to displace companies in a heartbeat. Case in point is Uber since a similar app can be created by anybody, Uber cannot hold the market for long and billions invested in Uber may be gone without a trace. Imagine a cooperative of drivers providing the same service developing an app which manages this service like Uber. The app cost is insignificant compared to driver cost and the drivers would get most of the benefit both as a shareholder in the cooperative as well as for providing the service. This dual income would become the norm in the new system and will significantly alter the way people would think about work and job.

The new system will provide huge opportunities for the workers but, the workers should transition to the new system with the following changes:

1. Learn about the new system and cooperative principles compared to corporate capitalism

2. Invest in the new system technology cooperatives

3. Based on the knowledge, skill and experience, find the role in the management of the cooperatives

4. Use the most important principle of cooperatives, one-person-one-vote for checks and balances

5. Be part of the new system organizations for protecting the rights

6. Pledge to share the knowledge and mentor this generation and next

7. Use the opportunity to do the work which you enjoy rather than just to earn a living

8. Stop being a victim and get involved for yours and community betterment

To summarize, the new system will make every worker in their sector an owner directly or indirectly. Direct ownership owning the land (agriculture), property, technology (they contributed) or any other assets. The indirect ownership is one being a shareholder in the cooperative which manages all these properties or assets. The initial amount or additional amount invested in the cooperative provides the opportunity to be an indirect owner. The income will be from ownership (direct or indirect) and from the work they do. If they cannot work anymore or cannot find work, the income will be only through ownership and if they work, it will be from ownership (dividends) and compensation for their work.

For example, a technology-cooperative formed by the workers in the technology sector will purchase or build technology tools to be used by the customers by paying a fee for it. The people who helped develop the technology or acquired from will be the direct owners. The technology tool acquired will be enhanced and maintained with the use of share capital of the members of the cooperative and the shareholders become indirect owners of these technology tools. When the income from these tools is derived, based on the ownership, the income will proportionately go to the direct and indirect shareholders.

In case of the agriculture cooperative, the landowners will have direct ownership on the land they own, and the inputs required for growing and the expenses of reaching this produce to the customer is facilitated by the share capital of both owners and the workers in the agriculture sector. When the income is derived from selling the produce to the customers, based on the ownership, the income will proportionately go to the direct and indirect shareholders. Also, the workers who helped in field, packing and processing, transport and delivery, will be paid their fair share of wages for their efforts. If the workers are not the direct owners, and cannot find work or cannot work, they will get income from the indirect ownership.

The present worker-exploitive capitalist system should come to an end and this new system must be adopted by the workers to have a steady basic income through ownership (direct or indirect) and then based on the skill, knowledge and the efforts put in by the workers, the work income can be derived.

The next ten chapters provide the structure required for each sector workers to adopt the new system and build the basic building blocks to derive the income.

PART 2

9

IT and IT-Enabled Services

Information Technology is quite a big part of the new economic system. In fact, it is the driving force for all the other sectors which require technology to be efficient and cater to the huge number of members or customers. This industry, which includes IT, computer and BPO sectors varies in size as a percentage of the country's GDP. In most countries, it varies from 2 to 10%. Ideally, it should be between 6 to 10%. The workforce in the sector includes the IT developers, hardware engineers, BPO and call-centre workers and should be in line with the percentage of GDP around 6 to 10%, but there is a huge gap even in the IT capital India. The workforce forms only 1 to 2 percent of the workforce whereas the industry revenue is 8 to 10% of the GDP.

The one country to study to see the optimal technology required for a country to be efficient and productive would be the USA. Every sector uses the technology required optimally; however, the benefit of this technology and automation does not go to the workforce. This will change once the technology is owned by the cooperatives and not by private companies. Even the poorest country in the world requires technology and support to be efficient and cater to all the people. for example, the healthcare sector requires doctors at every city, town and village to cater to the entire population. The poor countries do not have access and come to the city to get the required medical services. However, the technology of using telemedicine would allow doctors to reach every village without being physically present there. This provides the means required for the poorest of poor and villages to get access without making a trip to the city. The technology and cost of setting up a telemedicine centre at the village are minimal now, compared to the doctors physically reaching the villagers or villagers reaching the city hospitals. This is cost-effective, affordable, sustainable and the most important infrastructure required to serve the poor in remote places. But it does not mean that the entire profit from the telemedicine goes to the IT sector; it should be only a fraction—around 10%—and 90% should go to the doctors and service providers. This model makes sure that the technology is used and the various sector-workforces benefit from it.

Every sector needs technology which makes the life of the service providers easy and provides good-paying jobs if the technology is owned by people. The technology startup companies which are disrupting other sectors using technology and replacing people are the first companies to be stopped. For example, the *Expedia, MakeMyTrip* who have developed the website and interfaces to travel services, have in a big way, replaced most of the travel agents around the world and all the way making consumers do all the work of research good deals, finding the best prices and booking the tickets, all the while charging us for the so-called 'convenience fee'. These rentier technology models do not add value but extract most of the revenue from the people. If the technology-cooperative develops these applications and takes only a fraction of the revenue from it, the people working in those sectors benefit.

Organizations

Other than a few giant technology companies in the world, the next level companies are in micro, small and medium. The employees range from 2 to 100 in these companies. There are industry organizations like any other industries, but they conveniently ignore the small and medium companies when it comes to help them develop and market products or in providing services.

The companies are fondly known as 'start-ups' and unfortunately, they are wasting the national intellectual resources in many countries. The statistics are mind-boggling. 97% of the technology start-ups fail in the first year! Who in the right mind would think that they will be in the 3% and survive when most likely they will be in the 97%? There are more tech graduates than you think. Last year in the Silicon-Valley of India, Bangalore saw 7000 start-ups established and maybe most of them shuttered at the end of the year. But, why this madness when you know that most of them fail? The answer is, there is no choice. One, there are no jobs available for the graduates. Only 1 in 5 gets a 'job' not 'the job' aspired. The other option to self-employ would be to start a small company and there is no organization which guides them to make this effort productive.

The new system would provide the cooperative framework for these start-ups to manage and develop productive applications people can use and help them collaborate and make them into a large organization providing technology to people-centric organizations.

10

FOOD AND AGRICULTURE

My friend's father, a retired government employee was highly active in the stock market after his retirement. He used his retirement benefits and put it to work very successfully in the stock market. I asked him how he selects the stocks and how he has been so successful; he said, 'It is very easy: I invest only in food stocks. As people cannot survive without eating, the food-related companies will never go out of business.' It makes sense; the food industry would be the most profitable business, but, when we cannot live without food, and the farmer is the one who is producing the food, why is the farmer not on top of the world? Our system is set up to shortchange the most important person in the food industry. Everyone makes money but the farmer. This is one of the major sectors which need to be made equitable in the new system.

In India, agriculture and food were one of the most local organized sectors through cooperatives and organizations. But I do not know when the capitalists hijacked it and made it their own. The age-old formulae followed by mothers and grandmothers were repackaged and made into an expensive healthy food. The cooperative farming transformed into corporate farming with efficient logistics to deliver food across the country and across the world. Well, do we need the capitalists and corporates to manage our agriculture and food distribution? It is a big NO. It is time to regroup and bring the grass-root level organizations and cooperatives back, make the technology available to them to make them efficient to help the people to benefit.

India's agriculture cooperatives are well established and serving a large number of people. But, compared to the population, it is negligible. The biggest reason for it is that government interference and corruption in the pretence of helping the farmers have destroyed the sector. There are cooperative banks which are supposed to help the farmers, there are federations for every type of crops and livestock, but they have failed to make an impact due to the politicians controlling them and not updating themselves for last 60 years. The one bright spot is the milk cooperatives (Amul).

Amul is the most successful cooperative system which has been in operation for the last 70 years. The model has been used by almost all Indian states to base their milk generation, processing and distribution. The Amul model can be used for every agricultural sector with minor changes which will make it more efficient, reduce waste and increase the income for the farmers and everyone who is working through the supply chain. There is no part of the entire food supply chain that we require a corporate entity to add value.

The waste of food and food-related products is 30 to 40 %. It means that at the same amount of production, it can feed another 30 to 40 % of the population. So why not streamline the process, take it away from the warehouses, retail stores and streets and make it available to the consumers directly? It is possible if people work together and make it happen.

Production of agriculture goods especially in developing and poor countries is wasteful and not sustainable. The farmers are not able to produce quality products at a reasonable cost due to the smaller and smaller land ownership. The land across the developing and poor countries is divided substantially by the passing of each generation. They do not realize that the land of 10 acres does not become 5 acres each for the next generation of two children but, 10 percent less at every time the part of the land sold due to fencing and the space between the lands to be left for access. This not only reduces the land base but also increases the cost of produce and transport due to smaller size. So what is the solution for this: the cooperative farming among the adjacent smallholders making it more productive, less costly and more of quality products.

The products which are good for the cooperatives are every food type. But the way cooperatives would work for different products will be a little different. For example, the sugarcane crop does go to many cooperative sugar factories, but the farmers themselves do not produce in the cooperative way. The vegetables are something which are most wasted and most perishable items which require logistics and a distribution system like a just-in-time system but still can do it with the same vendors, hawkers and small merchants, but mobile and digital technology, instead of high cost online or big-box retailers and supermarkets.

The first level cooperative would be to produce the agriculture products in a collective.

Advantages:

♦ You can produce more per acre from 100 acres of land compared to 1-to-5 acres of land.

♦ The transportation cost is cheaper compared to small farms increasing the profits.

♦ Stress-free farming with proper insurance on yield.

♦ Use of modern technology in farming methods to increase quality yield.

♦ With cooperative managing the workers, equipment, fertilizers, the cost reduces drastically.

♦ Like milk cooperatives, the responsibility of the farmer's responsibility ends by delivering it to the processing stage.

There are four stages to the agriculture produce reaching the actual consumer:

1. Collaborative farming
2. Processing and packaging

3. Distribution

4. Delivery

Collaborative farming

The collaborative farming includes initiating the process joining together ten or more farmers preferably on adjacent lands. The cooperative is at village-level with multiple cooperatives possible in each village. The farmers along with the representative from federation will conduct seminars to bring everyone together explaining the procedure and the process involved. The seminar will include:

1. The process and procedure for the cooperative.

2. Roles and responsibilities of each member of the cooperative and federation representative.

3. The accounting, wages and other payments to the workers, equipment and fertilizers.

4. Sharing of profits as well as other benefits from the cooperatives like healthcare, education, etc.

Processing and packaging

This step involves grading, processing, packaging and storage. These are equivalent to the unions in Milk Federation. Once the grading and processing are done, based on the schedule, the products will be stored and then the required packaging is completed, and the product will be on its way to the consumer through the distribution cooperatives.

Distribution

The farmers are burdened with sale and distribution of agriculture products to the APMC yards, city food markets, stores or to hawkers who complete the cycle with last-mile-delivery. It is the most inefficient system and we are expecting farmers to know the market, arrange transportation and do financial transactions.

Farmers require professional support in distribution like the large Agri companies who create a seamless supply chain to reach their stores and supermarkets.

Technology helps in providing the same support to the farmers in the sale and distribution of products. Imagine that the farmer receives the order in advance as to the requirement in different markets with acceptable prices before he can load the products on to the truck. This will reduce waste and increase their income.

Delivery

The last-mile delivery of Agri products is still 80% through small stores and hawkers. It may seem fine to provide millions of jobs for the people who are providing last-mile to the consumers. But, the amount of food wasted through this system is colossal. You could see the vegetables sitting on the baskets at millions of small retailers or on the carts of the hawkers and rot. Also, the store owner and hawkers work from early morning to late night to earn a meagre amount after paying the microloan, interest and bribes they pay.

The solution is in organizing these hawkers and small retailers and providing them with the technology to receive orders and delivering the products as needed by the local consumers.

Imagine a system where the daily, weekly and monthly requirements of the family are collected online or by the local executive over a mobile device and conveyed to a database server which consolidates the orders for that area and procures the products for that area as required and delivers it to the store where it is segregated based on the order and the hawkers take the segregated products and deliver to the consumers in the area.

Using the technology available, the whole supply chain can be streamlined, and it will generate more jobs through a reduction in the wasted products. Also, it involves the same stakeholders giving them more income with half the work they were doing earlier.

11

ENERGY FOR FUTURE

Climate change is the biggest threat to mankind today. We cannot continue with the same unsustainable growth anymore. It may be true to some extent that a country's growth will be curtailed if restrictions are applied to the consumption of resources. But it is possible to reduce or eliminate waste from the system without curtailing the growth by developing and implementing efficient systems. Also, in the case of renewable energy, there is a role to play for the financial sector, but it will be people-centric for the most part.

The turnaround from fossil fuels to renewable energy should be the opportunity for the removal of corporates and the introduction of cooperatives and collectives. There are four aspects to energy: generation, transmission, distribution and energy efficiency.

One of the biggest reasons for not adopting renewable energy is the huge investment in thermal and other power plants by corporations. Whenever there is a debate on renewable energy and climate change, the corporations make sure that climate change itself is denied as a hoax and prevent any kind of progress in it. Also, the renewable energy market is controlled by them, making sure that it is not a viable source. But, the cooperative energy generation is the way forward to deter the corporates from hijacking this movement and Germany, with its thousands of cooperatives implementing solar, biofuel and wind energy, has given hope of replacing fossil fuels with renewables all over the world.

The generation part in the non-renewable (thermal mostly) is centralized for the economics of scale, but in renewable like solar or wind, it can be anywhere from localized on a rooftop to a centralized power plant. The low maintenance, as well as the natural fuel (sunlight and wind), make it the most suitable for future energy needs. The renewable energy generation moving forward should be totally cooperative-based and with an innovative financial model to make sure that most of the benefits go to the people rather than to corporates and the top 1%.

The transmission part of energy requires huge investment as well as agreements with thousands of landowners to lay the transmission lines and grid across the country. In most countries, it is a government or state enterprise which maintains the lines and should be the way for all the countries.

The financial model for renewable energy generation interestingly replicates the model used by the corporations in all their businesses. For example, if a company is starting a product line, the company's financial contribution would be about 10% and 90% is borrowed from banks or investors at a low interest rate of around 5 % to 6%. If a project is $100 million, only $10 million would be shareholder equity and $90 million would be in loans. The equity share may vary based on the risk of the project, but it does not cross 30%. If the project generates 20% gross profit, in our example, about $20 million a year, $10 million would go to paying off the principal and interest, and $10 million would be the revenue for the company. If 80% goes in expenses, there is still $2 million in profits for the shareholders at about 20% profit for $10 million investment. It is quite a healthy return. Imagine a cooperative uses a similar model in a Solar PV project and with 10% investment; the cooperative shareholders can make a healthy income from these projects. The example of a solar power plant is given below to illustrate the model which will indicate the type of model which can be developed and replicated all over the world.

Community renewable energy plant

An MW-scale solar power plant which uses the PV (Photovoltaic) technology is the simplest and most cost-effective solar power plant available today. It also the largest of renewable energy projects running at many Gigawatts around the world. The project involves laying out PV panels at certain angles in relation to the sun to get the maximum sunrays on them and the PV cells convert this solar energy into electrical energy. There are no moving parts, so no maintenance problems, but simply clean the surface of the panels periodically and check the wires, connectivity and monitor the power generation through remote monitoring tools. The technology has advanced over several years to increase the efficiency of the cells and the price of cells has come down dramatically in the last couple of years making it the most cost-effective solution. The generation efficiency reduces only 15 to 20% over its lifetime and the project lasts around 25 years. Thanks to global warming, almost all parts of the world are suitable for PV solar projects.

Most of the PV plants around the world are owned by corporates and some are community-owned. With the financing available at very low interest, large companies are enjoying the stable revenue from these power plants.

In the new economic system, every renewable energy plant should be owned by the community or cooperative in a local area. When the investment requirement is only 10% and 90% is provided by low-interest loans from banks, there is no need for corporates to own these renewable energy plants. If you take only PV solar plants, it is easy to install, need minimal maintenance and generate revenue without any raw material except the sun.

Every village, town or city resident can own the renewable energy plants by forming local cooperatives and enjoy the benefits for 25 years.

12

MANUFACTURING & INDUSTRIES

Manufacturing has changed significantly in the last 20 years. The idea of having a huge number of employees doing every work is obsolete. Automation has replaced most of the labour and if not automation, it is outsourced to low-wage countries. It is not a picnic for the workers in low-wage countries also. The child-labour and worker exploitation with inhuman working conditions have become the hallmark of corporates who are obsessed with reducing costs and increasing profits. The advertising is creating false demand to push the products and into western countries and most of the productivity gains are going to the large corporations.

The small and medium industries are not using the automation required to produce quality products and are not able to deliver quality products. Also, these small industry owners (most of the time proprietors or single owners) are burdened with arranging finances, managing administration, procuring raw materials, hiring skilled manpower, producing quality products and doing sales and marketing. Any large industry will have a huge staff that would be taking care of each department. The organization of these small and medium enterprises is supposed to help them in every aspect of SME industrial management. Even though the organizations exist, they are not doing what they are supposed to.

There are many organizations which are bringing together these micro small and medium industries. I studied deeply one major organization of a state with about two hundred thousand industries and it is quite pathetic as to how these organizations are run and represent their industries. The only major event in the year is the bitter elections for the governing body. Any change made by the previous body is undone in the next year and new irrelevant changes are made in the next year.

In the new economic system, the role of MSME organization will be more of a productive support system than just a lobbying organization. When we are talking about two hundred thousand industries in a state, we have to think of many things which can really change the way these industries operate.

The organization will be one which provides procurement support to reduce the input cost. It will help in production with skilled manpower and technology to produce quality products. And finally, provide market support to help them sell their products without incurring too much marketing costs.

Organized Industry procurement

The organization of industries should be in the foremost in helping the member industries to procure raw materials. The difference between the large company and small and micro industries is the way they procure raw materials. The SMEs pay a very high cost for the raw materials which results in higher cost of products or lower margins. A small change in the price of raw materials will put them out of business.

Skilled manpower and production technology

The skilled manpower tends to go to larger industries and when they do not get jobs there, they tend to prefer smaller companies. If the organization is strong and supporting the industries, the trend will change. Also, the organization would take the responsibility of skill-development and enhancement and provide the manpower required rather than SMEs themselves are burdened with the manpower management.

The technology and automation would reduce the work by workers and helps in producing quality products. But, the profit from the automation should be shared with the workers rather than replaced. This is a good quality of the industry which will be appreciated by customers and will increase sales.

Industry output

These hundreds of thousands of industries are producing products which are consumed by people or may be going as spares for large industries. An inventory of the output will give the range of products produced by these industries and it is possible to give a market for these products through online and other means. This reduces the uncertainty for the small industries, and they can concentrate on producing quality products.

The inventory of products also provides the means to weed out redundant and unnecessary products and helping them produce products which are necessary and based on the market requirement. Market support should be one of the primary functions of the small and medium industry organization.

The manufacturing industry is one of the major industries which provide jobs and products needed by the people of a country. It is not to say that every product should be produced in the country. But in the new economic system, the requirements go from local to global. Every industry which has to be local should be local and additional products should be procured from outside. The goal should be collaboration rather than competition.

13

MEDIA

———— ✍ ————

This topic is way up, above healthcare or education because of the importance of media in a democracy. Also, it is the most important information source for people in the time of fake news and corporate media which are distracting the whole media and the message. The information crisis is due to the corporate media which is in the news business just to make money. If sensational news is out there, the corporate media will compete with one another to get their news to be shown first. But, if there is no sensational news, they create the news from anything they can get their hands on and sensationalize it.

It is very easy to create fake news online through social media. It requires just a few people to keep forwarding to different groups they are part of and the fake news spreads all over the social media. The fake news cycle would stop after a couple of days if it is limited to the social media, but, in the corporate media depending on which political party they are supporting or the leaning of the corporate house which owns the channel, the fake news is given new wings and becomes mainstream. Even though this cycle ends in a week or so, the damage is done permanently. When it is discovered that it was fake news, there are no consequences to the mainstream media or social media for spreading false information and they do not need to apologize for it. There is a crisis of right information and news. There is a crisis of journalists becoming propaganda agents and thus giving rise to crony capitalism and corporates managing our government. This needs to be stopped and we need to get back to the time when the media is the fourth pillar of democracy and when the media questions every wrong policy taken by the government and provides people with the right information.

To start the process of media-reform and restoring media as the fourth pillar of democracy, the first step is to give the workforce of media a platform to earn their living without having to succumb to the advertisers, corporates or the politicians. This also means that the local news is given importance to give all the local journalists and media a platform for keeping a check on the local and state government and public information. The changes needed are immense, but it is not impossible. First, we create a common cooperative where everyone related to media is part of it. The cooperative will act as a common platform to provide the right information and journalism for the people.

Paying for the news should be the responsibility of the people to make sure we keep them true to their profession and give them a living wage to be effective in their profession. The subscription model for the print media as well as the online media (it is new-age TV media) and the subscription by the people is only by the quality of work.

14

TRANSPORT & TRAVEL

Travel and transport sector includes services in everything from local transportation, national and international transportation, hotel stay, and goods-transport. The travel and transport service industry is a multi-billion-dollar industry which used to employ a huge number of workers around the globe. It forms an important sector for the GDP of a country in providing a huge number of jobs and revenue. Even though the revenue from the sector is increasing rapidly, the jobs are eliminated substantially in the last few years as automation and technology are making the jobs scarcer. The travel and transport services which were provided by small and medium enterprises are going through a huge technology change with online travel booking, automated check-in and other technology tools. These tools controlled by the large corporations have used them to make these small and medium enterprises obsolete while making huge profits. The next revolution in self-driving cars is sure to scare the drivers into worrying about their future. Even though it is too soon to visualize the impact of this technology on a global scale, it is time to prepare and make the technology work for us rather than enrich the large corporates.

In most cases, the initial impact of technology was to make the lives of the service providers easy. A booking agent for a hotel had to literally, call every hotel to get the best deal demanded by the customer. But, the online portals provided all the information required like fares, options available and information about the infrastructure and service quality handy for the customers to choose from thousands of options. This choice and options were initially available with just a small commission which would not justify having a travel agent do the work for you. However, these small commissions were not enough for these corporates who started charging unsuspecting customers hidden fees and other penalties which amounted to more than the honest agent's fees which would have given these agents jobs and income. The jobs in all these technologies-enabled-services companies in travel and transport have reduced to a point where they need only a skeleton staff to manage these businesses across the globe. The customer service is almost non-existent, and these fraud and deceitful practices will continue unless people wake up and realize how these companies have hijacked the industry and are cheating people.

The local service providers did much more than just book the tickets or provide information. They were specialists who added value with their passion to travel or finding the best deals through the knowledge of the industry. The right transition to the technology would be to provide them with tools to make the bookings and other services easy to provide and to give them information to enhance their knowledge so that they can provide the best service to the people. However, the industry corporates chose a path which eliminates these jobs and passes the burden of acquiring knowledge about travel and transport to the customers in addition to paying huge commissions for these services. The customers who spend their time to get this information and made informed decisions were rewarded and those who did not, pay the penalty of paying higher prices and get crappy deals.

The customer-support services are literally non-existent in the travel and transport industry. The customers are on their own when they travel and need support when things do not go as planned. With self-online bookings or app-bookings, it is a luxury to have somebody from the service providers or booking sites on the phone to help. Even if by some luck, you get someone on the phone, the customer-support personnel are either ignorant or biased towards the company. It reflects in the way they have been trained to tackle pesky customers who persistently call to complain or request help without going through the website for answers. Anything which costs money for these corporates is considered going away from the goal of making money, including providing customer-support. They would rather be spending money to acquire more customers using advertisements and marketing calls than helping the customers who have already paid the money. This trend is going to be worse with huge competition in the industry and collusion between the service providers. The organization of consumers using these services is very much required to protect our rights and make sure that the service providers are held accountable for their predatory practices.

The app-based local taxi and other transport services have been touted as revolutionary when Uber and other app-based taxi providers entered the market. Instead of calling for the taxi, you must use an app, which was developed using an existing technology of GPS and other technologies. This app-based hailing cab is nothing innovative, but just a technology-enabled service which already existed as a radio-taxi service. The only difference was that the radio-taxi service required a human interface to book a cab and give directions for the taxi to arrive at the pickup point. The technology Uber uses, which can be developed by a few programmers, has been used to make commissions of 20 to 30% which is outrageous and predatory, exploiting the drivers and consumers to enrich themselves. The drivers who are in the Uber and other app-driven company networks must pay the commission, vehicle purchase expense, fuel and other maintenance for the vehicle and end up with less than 20% of the fare charged. While the model has not helped the service providers, it has also not helped the consumers. The driver unrest is seen in the type of service they are providing and the Uber response to this unrest and drivers legitimate demands is to experiment on using self-driving cars. This trend will turn out to be a disaster for everyone and create a mess in all the countries with the huge number of drivers and other service providers in the travel and transport industry losing jobs and income. The cooperative model for the travel and transport industry will be the most equitable solution and the new economic system cooperative model bring the customers, service providers together and make sure they get the services at reasonable prices as well as promoting local jobs and incomes to remove inequality.

The local commuter transport must look beyond the Uber and other service providers for efficient local transportation. The public transport which considers only buses, trains and other mass transportation options should include shared-transport and last-mile-connectivity transport as part of the overall transport requirements locally. The governments controlled by the corporates and other entities make sure that public transport is discouraged to help them sell more cars or individual vehicles. Otherwise, why would any city government not consider or design a comprehensive system which covers the entire length of the journey? There are also other forces which insist that public transport can be managed efficiently by private entities and lobby to shift it to the private sector. It is going to be a disaster! And it is never going to work with the making money as the only goal of the private companies. The cooperative sector which recognizes both the public or state-owned public transport, as well as the other requirements of shared and last-mile-transport, is the ideal solution. The cooperative will be the catalyst in bridging the gap in service between mass transport and other shared-service providers. It will make the public transport as well as the shared-transport efficient which would help the commuters, help the local transport service providers make a decent living as well as reduce the traffic with efficient use of transport options. Before solving the problem, we need to understand the problem the commuters are facing and not accept the charade of Uber type of shared-transport private solutions. The new economic system technology-cooperative will provide all the technology tools required for the commuter transport solutions and the travel and transport cooperative shareholders and employees will implement the comprehensive solution taking the existing public transport options into consideration and in partnership with the government.

Goods transportation includes long-distance transport as well as local transportation. The large logistics providers have perfected the service using the technology to their advantage. The movement of goods in the warehouse long-distance as well as local transport is completely controlled and monitored to reduce the travel as well as fuel which results in efficient transport. Walmart and Amazon boast of using very sophisticated technology to efficiently deliver goods and purchases to the consumers. However, most of the goods-transport is by the unorganized sector. Individuals or group of vehicle-owners as a small business provide the services in an inefficient way, wasting fuel with empty return trips, charging customers more to cover this waste but not making much money. To truly solve this problem, it is important to get these unorganized small businesses in goods-transport to bring them in a network and provide the digital infrastructure required to make them efficient and to help them make a decent living.

Travel and transport cooperative

The cooperative model should work both at the local and national level with service providers getting the most benefits. The new economic system cooperatives work exactly like the large logistics and transport providers for efficiency except for the cooperative principles. It is better to have one major cooperative federation for the country, networking all the local and state cooperatives operating as branches or franchises throughout the country. The branch or franchise makes sure that the process of working of the cooperative will not be reinvented and each local and state cooperative is efficient and does not waste the precious resources and finance in relearning. The inclusion of all the three types of travel and transport (national and international travel, local commute and goods-transport) into one major cooperative network as it provides the shareholder revenue from multiple sources to make sure that equitable income reaches the service providers.

The cooperative will follow a hybrid franchise model or branch of a large cooperative model based on the need. If the income is only from the local services, the franchise model is suitable. It can be seen in the local commuter services where they work only locally in a city and since the local cooperative franchise has a stake in the central cooperative federation, they get the secondary income from the royalties and other income at the federation level. The national and international travel cooperative will be one common cooperative throughout the country with branches in different local areas and states. This is due to the nature of the services provided to anybody in the country from any other place. The service providers will be benefitted not just from their local bookings but all the bookings in the country. Also, the local service providers have a dual role as the booking for other destinations as well as for being the service providers at their city.

Organizations

The organizations which support and use the cooperative services include both local transport users as well as the network of travel and transport users throughout the country. The local associations which need to be created or existing organizations strengthened are the commuter associations. The national and international travellers would be part of the network instead of a formal association. The goods-transport users may range from individual households to local and national companies and organizations which can work in a network environment better instead of the association.

The commuter association

Most of the travel in a city during peak hour when the traffic congestion is at its worst is done by the commuters going to work, business schools and colleges. In numbers, usually, they are 70 to 80% of the total vehicle population. The first step in finding the solution to the traffic congestion problem is to organize the biggest group of travellers, the commuters.

The commuters' association would represent the commuters in every respect—the rights of the commuters, liaison with government, employers, businesses, school and college management, traffic police and the transport department. The commuter association will facilitate different services required for the commuters like last-mile-connectivity, park-and-ride facilities, shared-transport and optimizing public transport. The affordability of commute is a major issue when different types of shared transportation are deployed; the commuter association would work with employers, government and other organizations in subsidising the shared commute through green tax, employer contribution, sponsorship, etc. The commuter association is the most important collective organization which will make the real difference in eliminating the traffic congestion.

The commuter association in each city and nearby suburbs will create an organization which will sincerely represent the commuters of that city. The stakeholders in the commuter organization are not just the commuters, but the government (all related), service providers (drivers, training schools and others), traffic police, businesses and employers. All the stakeholders should work together to make sure that the biggest problems—traffic congestion and pollution—are solved.

Travel & transport Network

The travel-booking-service is done at a national level and the requirements of these services are sporadic and people need support and help only when they transport. However, the requirements of customer-support and help while travelling is greater than local transport. But, since the travel is arranged by the cooperative, a sizeable amount should be kept aside for the customer-support to distinguish from the other private service providers and make sure the users are automatically in a network while on road to give them peace of mind and wonderful memories of the travel.

The goods-transport is mostly accessed by private companies and local firms. The network of the users will help them in accessing these services efficiently and cost-effectively. The biggest problem in goods-transport is vehicles making the return trip empty. If the users' network is comprehensive, the wasted return trips can be utilized, and the overall service becomes cheaper. With this network, the users who use the small and medium service providers can get the same or better customer service from these small firms compared to the large logistics providers.

Technology & support

The technology-cooperative will provide all the technology, customer-support and back-office support for the travel and transport industry cooperative. If the technology is not developed, the tech-cooperative will source it from IT companies and provide everything needed for the most efficient running of the industry cooperative. The basic IT tools required would be:

a. Cooperative management system—The cooperative shareholders, employees, contractors, partners, finances, legalities and compliance are managed using a comprehensive Information management system. All the necessary tools, both online and mobile, should be available to the cooperative management to manage with transparency. The shareholders will get the necessary information about the progress of the cooperative, about their dividends, voting requirements and will be able to give and receive feedback, complaints, concerns as well as suggestions and advice. This management system is the most essential software system for the new economy cooperative.

b. Finance, banking and insurance—The finance, banking and insurance management system is a common software system for any industry-specific cooperative. The payment gateway, mobile wallet, finance management and insurance management software systems are developed or acquired by the technology-cooperative and services provided by the common finance, banking and insurance cooperative.

c. The local shared-transport, public transport and taxi services need a comprehensive online application as well as an app, which helps the commuters and service providers to communicate, provide information and facilitate the use of sustainable transport. All the service providers will be part of the travel and transport cooperative.

d. The travel portal and app will connect to the travel service providers like buses, trains, cabs, rental cars, airlines and hotels and other stay options. The travel and transport cooperative will manage the listings in their own city and be the point of contact for the national and international travellers.

e. The goods-transport management system will register all the partner small and medium service providers as well as manage the transportation services using technology like GPS and maps.

f. All the purchasing of vehicles, spares and other products and services required for the travel and transport industry, like vehicles, spare parts, insurance, etc., are facilitated for the shareholders through the online portal managed by a cooperative which will utilize the group-purchasing-model to get the best prices and quality products. The consumer cooperative which would manage this portal would do thorough research on the quality of the product and get the best prices.

g. Finally, the Phapa Messenger app will facilitate communication between the various cooperatives, service providers, members and the service users. It will help in creating a network based on different sectors, and link to the cooperative administration and service providers to get the information and support.

15

EDUCATION

The conventional school, college and university education has survived for centuries. The schools are teaching to a group of children, one curriculum, irrespective of each one's capability to learn. The same thing happens in colleges and universities. Nobody is ready to change the system or think about a better system. Meanwhile, the children are struggling to cope with the rigours of this broken system while the parents struggle to finance these disoriented education programmes. The education programmes at each level are themselves in disarray in terms of preparing students for future careers.

In most of the countries, the schools and colleges started as public institutes run by the government with almost free education. As the population increased, private enterprises saw it as a great business opportunity and started spreading their tentacles everywhere. The private institutes charging exorbitant fees had to justify it by providing quality education, much better than public institutions but, they preferred to reduce the quality in public education through lobbying for legislation which reduced funding to the public schools. This phenomenon is seen everywhere including the US and a developing country like India.

The US public education is under constant threat through misinformation propaganda from private school lobbying and with the reduced funding, this will affect the quality of education and destroy public education unless measures are taken to counter them. It is surprising that a developing country like India has embraced private school education more than many other countries. The government schools are ignored to the point where the infrastructure and quality of education are deteriorating. Since most of the students attending school in government schools are poor, the dropout rates in these schools are very high. Opportunities for poor students for their future careers will be limited and the inequality between the rich and the poor will continue to increase. Even though the private schools are charging exorbitant fees and education quality is not up to par, people have a perception that the private schools are better.

One bright spot is the Delhi state government schools. The proactive Delhi government has done a remarkable job in resurrecting the government schools with good infrastructure as well as curriculum upgrade. The students in these schools are happy and getting a good education. This should be a model for the rest of the country.

The grades and evaluation system for students and schools are outdated and schools are misusing them and making them the prime focus of their goal rather than a good education. One ridiculous and illegal trick the private schools follow and get away in India, to get a better result in board exams is to remove the low-performing students from school before the board exam. When one of my relatives told me, I could not believe it. The government law prohibits the schools from doing this kind of activity; the parents blame their children for not studying and getting low grades. This is not an exception but the rule in many high-ranking schools around the country. This is possible only because the parents do not have the organization to protect them from these predatory practices of private schools.

The public schools which are financed by the government have more experienced and qualified teachers than the private schools, but without proper monitoring, the government teachers slack, and it affects the children's education. The parents of the children studying in the government schools think that getting free education is a privilege and one should not question the system. It is necessary for them to realize that it is a right and government works for the people and the teachers are paid by our tax money.

The system needs a major overhaul to function in a way that it works for all people. The predatory practice of the profit-oriented institutions should be curbed and even if the parents prefer private schools, the rights of those children should be protected. The new system should improve infrastructure and education in the government or public-school system to provide quality education at par with the private schools so that the opportunities for the poor children increase for their future career.

The new system will work complementary to the present education system in enhancing the education the students receive. Also, it helps in reducing the cost of education to make it affordable to everyone. Like schools, colleges and universities should be made affordable or free. This can happen only with a concerted effort by all the stakeholders in the education system.

The following steps are needed to make the new education system work for everyone:

1. Organize Parent-Teacher-Association at school, district, state and central level. For colleges and universities, student organizations at college, district, state and central level

2. Information system to provide guidance for educational choices.

3. School and college management participation in both public and private by parent and teacher representatives

4. Tutoring support at all levels for students who require additional help, using technology tools (e-learning, online and onsite)

5. Innovative Career-oriented training using technology tools and online/onsite model.

6. Job portal to facilitate career choice for job-seekers.

Education-related organizations

Parent-Teacher-Association in the US and other developed countries has been established as a norm in all the schools. But, their responsibilities and authority are limited and there is no way of parents or even teachers contributing to the improvement of the system. Also, with the PTA limited to the school, there is no way of communicating to other PTA from other schools in the district, state or centre. In the US, during the financial crash of 2008, many school districts were affected by the reduced revenue to the local, state and federal government. Many school districts reduced teachers and the number of school buses apart from many other cuts. The students coming from remote areas of the district had their bus-stop eliminated and many parents had to drive their children to the nearest bus-stop which was miles away. The frustrated parents raised the issue in the PTA, but the school management said, it was a district-level decision and they had no control over it. One parent took the initiative to unite the parents from different schools through social network and made sure that a network was created for the district and combined voice was raised to issues at the district-level, but the organization died down after the school year when the students graduated. The problems do not stop there and some of the issues are beyond their control and must be addressed by the state government or central government. The representation is very important when you look at the education-head in the US government who hates public schools and in the Indian government where an allegedly fake-degree-holder is the education minister. The example just provided the type of organization required to protect the interest of the children whose future depends on the education and environment provided in the school.

The college and university where the 18+ age students study must have their own student organization which protects their rights. Again, the organization limited to specific colleges is of no use. It should be at district, state and central level. The concept of political parties having their students' wing is not a healthy organization. The organization which takes care of the students' interest should be only one. The committee members can change, but there must be only one organization representing all the students. As student organizations, we are not preparing for the state and central politics. The students' manifesto is common no matter who is elected. The persons elected should just implement the manifesto. The idea of different parties competing in elections in the universities is just muddying the water and not protecting the interests of all the students. Just think about the left vs. right debate in one of the most prestigious universities in India, the Jawaharlal Nehru University (JNU). The ruling political party with their student-wing created fake propaganda about the student president and jailed him for sedition charges. These types of things happen all the time in campuses around the world where protest is considered a threat to the ruling party and if only at the college or university level, it will be curbed easily, but, if it is at the state and national level, the power of the people will be enormous.

Ideally, the government should be representative of all the different sectors. The education department of the government should be representative of the parents, teachers and students. It must cater to the needs of these stakeholders and no one else. The private school and university managements having lobbying efforts to swing the legislation in their favour is undemocratic. The lobbying into the education system in the US has gone to such an extent that apart from influencing for the type of education provided to the children, they have lobbied to classify pizza as a vegetable and can be served in school cafeterias. There is one thing which needs to be understood: The nexus between the corporate and government is catastrophic to our children and their future. If the parents were part of the decision-making process, do you think they would allow sugary drinks and unhealthy food? Even if some parents do not care or are ignorant about it, the majority-rule would make the right decisions, and everyone must comply and that is how democracy works. If the same decisions are left to the legislatures influenced by corporate interests, they will completely ignore the health of children and make decisions favouring themselves. The public opinion process for them is only to influence people through advertisements and false news with fake statistics. If the parents really want a change, they better participate in the process and protect the rights of the children and themselves.

If the government is not representative of the people, especially the parents of the school children, this cat-and-mouse game is going to continue until there is nothing else left to recover. The parents and teachers should be part of the agenda and manifesto of government and they should be the one making the decisions which affect the children. There is no room for profit-making institutes in education, but if the parents prefer that, high regulations should control the workings of these institutes with only limited profits. In many countries, the most compromised cost by private institutes is the salary of teachers. In India, you will find unqualified teachers who do not pass basic tests in their own subjects. It is because qualified and experienced teachers are discouraged due to low pay and even though they enjoy teaching, they work in other professions. The management of both public and private institutes should be by the stakeholders rather than profiteers. These changes are possible only if there is an organization at school, district, state and central level.

Online-classroom tutoring

Many students find it difficult to follow the standardized teaching methods. There are many technology-assisted programmes which can be used to improve the in-class teaching itself like the 'Khan Academy' which is doing a tremendous job by designing the in-class process to include everyone with different capabilities. It helps the teachers pay more attention to the students who require more help. But, it requires retraining the teachers and use of computers and technology in class which may not be available in most parts of the country due to the cost. However, in-class teaching can be enhanced for the students with after-school programmes using online/onsite hybrid model.

The availability of good teachers in different parts of the country differs based on the cities, towns and villages. This affects the outcome of the students' learning and, with the in-class standardized teaching not catering to all the students effectively, the after-school programmes play a significant role in bringing all students to a higher level of learning. The online learning will help in accessing the best teachers to teach from anywhere using live video classes. The online-only classes which require a computer and high-speed internet connection at home restrict the students to cities in many countries. The hybrid model works with a classroom with capabilities to conduct online classes, either using the existing infrastructure in schools and colleges or having small infrastructures outside to bring the nearby students from villages and small towns to utilize the teaching by qualified and experienced teachers from around the world.

Career-oriented training

The conventional schools and colleges are offering courses which may not be enough to prepare the students for the career opportunities available. The job-marketplace is changing rapidly due to technology and other factors, but the curriculum does not keep up with it as it takes several years to modify the course content. This is leaving a huge number of job-seekers ill-prepared for the jobs they would be doing. There is a huge need for preparing the job-seekers to provide short-term training which helps them to prepare for a successful career.

Again, the online/onsite model is the only model which will work for the career-oriented training. The online training provides that the students sit at home and go through the training which eliminates one important requirement, i.e., interaction with their fellow job-seekers. Career training is more than just learning new skills or enhancing their skills. It requires additional soft skills of language, communication, and many more life-skills which are essential for job-seekers especially from small towns and rural background. The training classroom provides with not only access to the teachers with industry experience and teachers with successful careers but also, interaction and exchange of ideas with their peers.

Mentoring for entrepreneurship.

In addition to the career-oriented training, the job-seekers, as well as small entrepreneurs, require all the help they can get to start a successful career. The future of work involves more of worker-owner type of enterprises or cooperatives rather than just a working career. When worker-owner kind of jobs requires more skills than just job skills, as an owner of a cooperative, you may have to wear different hats to have a successful business. The basic workings of the cooperative, accounts, sales and marketing etc., must be learned to participate in the cooperative business. This requires again, knowledgeable and experienced mentors who can guide the worker-owners. The notion of just knowing the tricks of the trade and then being on your own is the scam the capitalist has played with entrepreneurs for a long time. This is a boom-and-bust-model where a few businesses work and a few fail just to continue the waste in the system. Rather, the mentors should guide them throughout the business as long as they need help. The new cooperative enterprises will be replicable and work on the complete support for the successful stable business for a long time.

The rapid change in the work environment requires proper guidance in the career also. Many times, the job-seekers are lost in a maze of information which is confusing and hearsay which will have long-term implications. Take the case of the job opportunities in certain cities. The job-seekers rely on a lot of misinformation which says there are thousands of jobs available in a city. They would not think about the salaries, cost of living and other factors which, if not properly considered, will end up as a bad decision for life. Also, there are many options available to a graduate from a field. The job-seekers need mentoring in choosing the type of career and knowing all the options available to them. The mentor-network will help in many aspects of the career choices in the new system.

These features of the new system are available sporadically in various forms in various countries. If a sustained economic system must be developed, these should be implemented everywhere in a holistic model for everyone to use it. The potential for job opportunities in the educational organizations, network, tutoring, training and mentoring is enormous. These are all jobs created locally with good pay for the future generation. The technology should be as a tool to provide new opportunities and not to replace the workforce. Even if it replaces the workforce, the benefits of it should go to the people rather than corporates and the rich.

Franchise Education-related cooperative

Like all other sector cooperatives, the education cooperative also should be a franchise-cooperative at the district-level and network to link the cooperative at state and centre-level. The technology required to manage the education system is provided by the technology-cooperative and managed like a franchise. This standardizes the system and can be replicated and implemented anywhere without any growing pains.

The first cooperative required is for the teachers and educators. The contract teachers and other education-related service providers will be the employees of the cooperative to get the healthcare and other social security benefits. The school and college teachers can have additional income through online/classroom training and tutoring opportunities from the cooperatives.

The organizations of the new system should protect both the teachers and students from exploitation. Education should be a public institution and the right to education should be a fundamental right.

16

Consumer Products and Services

A few years back, I was in Dubai representing my company to provide a solution to a large consumer-electronics dealer. This company was part of a large group and the chairman of the group was supposed to come and attend my presentation. The presentation was in the boardroom and about 12 people were there and each one had his own water bottle placed on the table. The chairman entered and sat at the head of the table and the moment he looked at the water bottle he was furious, and he took the bottle and threw it in the trash can. He waited for everyone to be seated and asked his company people, "Why do you think I threw that bottle in the trash?" No one from his own company answered the question and I told him, "Because it is from your competitor." He got up and shook my hand and said, "It is sad that our own company people do not know that I have a water bottling company and my own companies use my competitors' water?" I did get the project, but it is a very important lesson for us: the consumers to know how the corporations procure products and services.

The corporations have teams of procurement experts who do all the purchasing for them. This is one place where the managements obsessively think about saving money. The procurement experts work with their own company's products first and then do thorough research to find the best products for the use of their employees and for their purpose. Are they swayed by the advertisement? Never. They know from their own company's advertisement that it is just a marketing tool and has nothing to do with the quality of the products. The procurement experts not only look at the quality and cost of the products; they look at what they can get out in sales for their own products. We the consumers are the only idiots who fall for the advertisements and manipulative sales and marketing practices. We buy stuff which we may not use more than once in its lifetime. We religiously keep buying all new products introduced irrespective of whether we need it or not. We are obsessed with companies with fancy brand names and ready to pay an exorbitant amount for products which we hardly use. We buy useless warranties which we have no idea how to use. We are not concerned that there is no repair shop even for the products under warranty in the 100-mile vicinity. Are we really this dumb or are we being played by the conmen from the corporation? There is no clear answer to it but we are not bright people. If not for this mental limitation, why would a person buy a car shelling out 30% of their salary in car-payments in cities like Mumbai, Bangalore, etc., where the average speed of vehicles is 5 to 10 Kms during peak hours? It really does not make sense. Looking at the economic situation around the world, I am sure that all these things will come crashing once people run out of money or all sources of loans (credit cards, second mortgages) are exhausted.

Consumers are being conned by the corporations only because of one thing: People are not organized. If we are organized as a group and buy only the things which need, we would have more money to spend on things which give us happiness or would be more financially comfortable in life. Also, for the products we need, we cannot buy as individuals. We must buy it as the corporates do collectively and only products we need rather than be swayed by the advertisements.

Organized group-purchasing and group-services is the only way the local-to-global shift can be achieved. The requirement for the products and services is initiated based on the local requirements. The wish-list of requirements would be converted into a group-purchasing programme and procured based on the requirement rather than the other way around.

Group-purchasing is the way the corporates buy their products and save. People, on the other hand, go to the store and buy retail. It is not just more money people pay for the products. It is the customer service, warranty and repair which costs us much more. As I mentioned earlier, being an individual consumer and trying to fight the company for faulty product or repair during warranty is a Herculean task.

The consumer organizations in the new system would not fight the corporates after the fact but in changing the laws to help the consumers get quality products and services. The consumer courts are set up to discourage people to fight for their rights. It requires people as individuals to spend their time and money to get justice. As far as corporates are concerned, they go by the statistics. They would settle one pesky consumer who tries to sue them in consumer court. The consumer organization should be proactive in every way. They should look at the quality of products, pricing and type of agreement we sign and protect the consumer in every step of the way.

17

HEALTHCARE FOR ALL

Single-Payer system is one of the most efficient systems for a country. But, with the disparate private and public health service providers, it is difficult to bring everyone on the same platform. Also, with the benefits of efficiency, advancement in healthcare technology and innovations going to only private companies and their shareholders and not helping the patients or healthcare workers, it is high time to change the system.

The new healthcare system should promote the incorporation of eco-friendly practices into healthcare delivery through information, preventive education, and service management in a cooperative model. The new healthcare system will strive to remove inefficiencies and waste from the system through the application of technology and provide the patients with access to affordable and efficient healthcare.

Currently, the different stakeholders (doctors, hospitals, diagnostic centres, pharmacies, and other healthcare service providers) do not work together due to the inherent disparities. The disparities range from inadequate digital infrastructure to seamless communication. Also, the lack of information and education is a serious impediment to the efficient delivery of healthcare.

With the inefficiencies and waste in the system, healthcare has become expensive and hassle-filled for consumers. Finding the right service provider who can match their need and budget is a Herculean task. Information and education on preventive care are literally non-existent or not accessible. There is a need for seamless collaboration and communication between all the stakeholders in the healthcare industry and to provide authentic information and education to the consumers. Also, there is a need for a system integrator who can bring these entities together and spearhead the collaboration.

Healthcare system has designed and developed efficient systems and tools which encompasses every stakeholder in healthcare, and which integrates the disparate entities in the healthcare industry to save money, time and hassle in healthcare delivery.

Healthcare system is managed by a team of dedicated professionals from various healthcare-related fields. The team is carefully chosen to address every aspect of the new healthcare paradigm healthcare is proposing.

There are three entities which form the Everything-People healthcare.

1. Patient organization or network

2. Cooperative of healthcare services

3. Healthcare payer—government or private

Patient organization or network

Patient health is the only reason the entire health industry exists. Patient as an individual is the most inefficient way for healthcare delivery. The misconceptions created by private service providers and insurance companies have increased the cost of healthcare exorbitantly in the US and many other countries.

Patients as individuals have no rights. The patient as an individual is exploited and pays the highest cost for healthcare. As a group, the patient is secured and will be able to get the quality healthcare needed at an affordable cost. The individual will be part of the network and different groups based on the geographic location, doctors and service providers accessed and also based on the chronic diseases to access the right information.

Healthcare cooperative

The healthcare cooperatives are essential for healthcare which will be the most effective facilitator of healthcare services for the people. With the maze of private and government healthcare programmes available in many countries, healthcare cooperatives will facilitate affordable and ethical care.

Also, with the advent of innovative healthcare technology, better drugs and better services, the cost benefits should go to the patients and service providers; instead, they go to the corporates and insurance providers. With the cooperative system turning service provider, this will be curtailed, and the benefits will go to the right people.

1. Service Provider management—Doctors, nurses and other service providers often work independently, as an employee or consultant. The requirement and the available resources often do not match. Also, even as employees, they do not get benefits like retirement, insurance, etc. If they are part of the cooperative organization, the service providers can build their career and other professional activities as a group.

2. Healthcare facility management—The clinics, nursing homes, hospitals and geriatric-care need professional management to provide affordable healthcare to patients. The profit-oriented private management companies which have a goal of only making money, will compromise the patient care and make the healthcare unaffordable. The cooperative with the technology and support services will be the most suitable for the management of facilities.

3. Third-party administrators—The insurance companies and government programmes require a third-party administrator to administer their programmes for their clients. The healthcare cooperative is the best suited to act as third-party administrators.

4. Pharmaceutical collaboration—With the hundreds of thousand drugs in the market and with patents and generic drug maze, it requires an independent entity which will make the care providers with the right information for the drugs to be prescribed. This

service will be provided with the technology and information collected at national and international level.

5. Telemedicine—facilitating telemedicine with the latest technology in communication reaching the most remote parts of the country to make the healthcare available to everyone.

6. Education programmes—create and provide education programmes in the preventive management of chronic diseases for better health management. Also, education programmes for healthcare service providers to improve care.

7. Patient health and medical records management digitally to make it available to healthcare providers for better healthcare delivery.

Healthcare Payer—Government or private

In most of the countries, healthcare cost is borne by government, private insurance (through employers), donors or the patients themselves. With the varied healthcare service providers, drugs and other products related to healthcare, it is difficult to manage the care efficiently. With the combination of patient-network and service-provider-cooperatives, healthcare will be streamlined. Even if the country decides to go for a single-payer system, these entities will be the most effective.

The new healthcare system will be a fraction of what is spent in the US (17% of GDP) and still be more effective and have healthy people rather than people suffering due to cost which is the major reason for the bankruptcy.

The simple process of healthcare access will be:

1. Everyone will have a health check-up every year and EMR created for future doctor reference. This will be done by health workers with basic science diploma and technology assists this process very much. There are health check-up kits which are portable and can be handled with basic knowledge.

2. Based on the outcome, there should be preventive support, primary doctor consultation or chronic disease support. But, before any action, there should be the completion of the next step

3. Everyone is assigned a primary healthcare service provider. The PHC doctor would be accessible either in telemedicine or PHC. The access to primary healthcare professional will be in most cases telemedicine and a few occasions at Primary Health Clinic.

4. The referral specialist and the consultation would also be telemedicine-process with the assistance of the primary healthcare doctor or nurse and the specialist would write the diagnostic tests to be done.

5. The EMR and the diagnostic tests would be used to determine the future course of action and the medicine to be taken or any other surgery, etc. to be done.

6. The medicine and other prescriptions would be through group-purchasing and delivery. The cost of medicine reduces by 40% when purchased through group-purchasing and there is no role of retail medicine shops in the new system.

7. Management through the disease would be proactive monitoring by healthcare support service providers and escalated to primary healthcare and specialist based on the condition immediately.

8. From the first step, if chronic diseases are identified, the chronic disease management is done on group-services. By design, these require constant monitoring and periodical testing which needs to be done as a group which is efficient.

9. The question of who pays for the healthcare services would be something countries need to answer soon. The government spending a certain percentage of GDP on healthcare is crucial and the tax on employers and other stakeholders should be considered. The basic efficient infrastructure is required for a country to take care of the healthcare need of the citizens.

10. There is no place for profit-businesses and companies to run healthcare and they will not be one of the stakeholders in the healthcare ecosystem.

18

FINANCE AND INSURANCE

The finance and insurance are the most skewed sector in terms of inequality of income to people versus capital. The ratio of income-to-finance workers in the sector versus investors or top management would be around 10-to-90. This was inevitable given the automation and technology developed in the past 25 years for replacing workers in this sector. Initially, there was no conspiracy in the automation as well as Information Technology use in the banks and other financial institutions, but after tasting blood, in getting the efficiency in services using technology, the sector went ballistic in making everything automated by online and mobile technology.

The use of Information Technology or software to manage the banks is the best way to efficiently manage, but the fruit of this efficiency going only to a few is the problem. If you look at the banking over the years, without technology, each branch would have been managing 400 to 500 customers with around ten employees. When the customers grew to 4000–5000, they would have needed 100 employees to manage them. But, the more-employees-to-more-customers was not sustainable or efficient; so technology was very much required so that millions of people can get service efficiently. Today, you can pay all the bills online, get cash from ATMs, deposit money or cheque at ATM or with mobile and you don't need the physical bank at all. Also, customer service would probably be talking to a machine. So, in terms of line-employees in a bank branch, it is an end-game for them. Now, if all the work which the tellers and other bank employees were doing is done by customers, then should not the bank be paying the customers from the enormous profit they are making? Well, they do not.

So how to turn around this skewed economic model; is it even possible? Well, it is not easy but, it can be done only if people understand the need and urgency to do it. The easiest way is to create and use cooperative banks for their banking, loans and other needs. There are already lots of credit unions and cooperative banks available but, people don't see the urgency. There is an outrage whenever there is a banking scandal; people go on Facebook and tell their friends not to use that bank, but nothing happens physically. Take the example of Wells Fargo bank: The employees were pressured so much to add new customers that they created millions of fake bank accounts, credit card accounts, etc. But nothing significant happened except that the employees lost their jobs and the CEO left with a golden parachute. You cannot change the system with this kind of lacklustre response. However, I do agree that unless there is a robust option available, and people are comfortable with it, the change will not happen. So, it is important to first analyze the banking sector, and create new or modify the existing to provide robust alternative and then it will be easy to pursue people.

Let us start with the purpose of the banks to the common people. A bank needs to keep our money safe, provide us with tools to deposit money, withdraw money, transfer money or pay for buying products and services, and use the money to provide loans to businesses or to people for buying high-ticket items. In no circumstance, the bank can use the deposited money other than in providing loans to the businesses and people. However, the banks do use the deposits as leverage and borrow more money and profit from it. So basically, the banks are borrowing 10 to 100 times the deposits they have and profit from it. Also, they would risk our deposits by their greed. This could be seen during the crash of 2008 when most of the big banks were insolvent due to huge losses and debt. The Obama administration had two options; one, to close the banks and pay the customers through the FDIC or second, shore up these banks with more money at 0% interest and help them come out of this situation. Well, the first option was unattainable as the FDIC would have to be shored by the government due to the huge amount of deposits to be paid. The FDIC wouldn't have sustained the bank-run and would have ended up in chaos. The government chose the second option which was the sensible one at that time, but not controlling them later and not prosecuting the culprits was the biggest mistake. Anyhow, it is time the people take the right action and make sure that these big banks are punished for their mistakes where it hurts—their bottom-line and profits.

First, to hurt their profits, we need to know where and how they make profits. It is not a vendetta we are doing when I say hurt their profits, but it means that it is important to know where they are making profits and then it can be diverted to us, the people, through smart banking changes. In most banks, their profits come from:

1. Transaction fees

2. Interest from loans

3. Interest from credit cards

4. Fees and penalties

5. And other God-knows-what transactions.

The first three are the ones which can be diverted using local banks, technology and customer power. The next two are eliminated if the first three are effective.

The fees and penalties, believe it or not, have become the bread and butter for the banks in the past few years. Even though with the concerted efforts of Elizabeth Warren, some of the fees were removed, they have still found a workaround and make money from it and get most of the revenues. This just needs to be eliminated and save the people money as it affects people in poor and lower-middle-class than others.

Banks have profited the transaction fee in collusion with the likes of VISA, MasterCard, etc. from our own money. The transaction fee for swiping debit or credit card is charged @ 2 to 3% when the cost of the transaction is less than 0.1%. This is ridiculous considering how long this has lasted. It was possible only because customers do not feel the pain as it is charged to the retailers and service providers. However, following suites from large retailers like Walmart, Sears, etc. against VISA and MasterCard brought to light the outrageous fees. With the mobile revolution, the players changed but the problem remains. But, with the right use of technology, it can be reversed, and the profits can go to the people instead of the big banks and credit card companies.

The loans were designed to purchase high-ticket items like homes and cars which cannot be purchased by saving for it. However, the loans for purchasing even a mobile phone is going too far and just make people buy stuff which they cannot afford or don't need. Back in the day, the cost of home phone and communication cost less than 1% of the average salary, but now, it may take more than 5% for the mobile phones and connectivity. This is mainly due to frequent change of mobile devices purchased on loan and paying through the nose for it. It is ridiculous to see people standing in line all night to buy a new device. The loans for these frivolous things should go.

The home loans are necessary and should be based on the affordability of the borrower. The subprime mortgages were designed to help everyone to get the opportunity to buy a home, but banks went too far in providing loans to people who cannot afford it and ended up creating the mess for everyone. The whole scam could have been avoided if the banks had stuck to the purpose and good faith for which the system was designed. But, one important aspect which is not highlighted in the whole mess was the builders did not build the houses (smaller) houses for the people for whom the system was designed.

The car loan is another monster which is out of control. The car loan is a big burden on families, and they end up buying cars which they cannot afford or need due to these 0% and 1% loans. There is no such thing as 0% on the huge amount of money they are giving to buy cars; it is being subsidized by the car companies by inflating the prices.

So, what can be done to eliminate these predatory practices, too large to fail banks and their conniving ways to make money from unsuspecting people? It is simple: Build the parallel system which works on democratic principles; it is people-friendly also as people generate income from it. The last part is important as generating income for people should be the priority as the profits which the big banks will lose should be the income to the people in terms of work in investment-income.

The new system for financial, banking and insurance system would be completely managed by people for the people. It would be distributed, decentralized and depict the existing banking except for the profits going to the people rather than to the investors.

The new system should serve the people of the community for their needs of banking, insurance, finance and other related services. The system should provide income to the community through profits or by employment. The investors in the system will be the customers, employees or workers, or local businesses. It should be self-sustaining, efficient and low-cost. There is no need to re-invent the wheel for the working of the financial system as the folks in the present banking system have already designed it.

19

REAL ESTATE & CONSTRUCTION

The real estate and construction businesses are one of the most unequal business models. The builders and speculators make huge sums of money while the workers are paid low wages. The nexus between the government and these real estate companies is one of the major reasons for this inequality as the huge tracts of land are given to not only the builders but to other sector industries also for throw-away prices by our government representatives on the pretext of developing industries and providing jobs. However, the builders, speculators and companies make the most money by exploiting the workers. The options available for the representative government would be to monitor and regulate the industries and builders to have a fair exchange of land and other subsidies by making sure that the workers get their fair share of the wages and profits from this industry which is a very important part of the economy.

The banks and financial institutes have entered this market in a big way by providing loans to the homeowners and builders to expedite the construction and home-ownership. But the banks have shown time and again that they are not satisfied with the pittance of loan interest they get and financialized the industry into securities and other financial instruments to speculate and bet on it to make huge profits. The huge profits also carried huge risks which led to the great crash of 2008 and the global financial collapse. The biggest victims were the homeowners who lost their homes and people who lost their jobs, but the banks came out unscathed when the government bailed them out with taxpayers' money. The notion of homes and other buildings being assets and investment has led to boom-and-bust cycles and the ultimate victims are the homeowners and potential homeowners.

The other part of the construction in building nation infrastructure used to be in the hands of the government, but it turns out, the financiers and banks have exploited and cornered most of the gains from these projects through public-private partnership and toll-based model. When President Trump announced that the US government will spend one trillion dollars for infrastructure, the workers in construction businesses got excited that finally a scheme like a new deal will propel the economy and help the struggling construction workers. But, the structure of the 'Deal' would be such that everyone accepts the workers and the local population will benefit. The financiers will fund the projects in anticipation of collecting tolls for years, the large equipment-manufacturers will sell their equipment at exorbitant prices and the builders and construction companies will bag the projects and make huge profits. Meanwhile, the construction workers will get a pittance working in some places which are not automated. The new improved deal will just enrich the already rich people and the local population will end up paying a toll for their lifetime while the bankers, financiers, company management and investors will fly over them in their private jets laughing all the way to the bank. This scenario is not a fiction or conspiracy theory but, a bitter reality which is already happening in all the countries even some of the poorest of them.

The solution is very simple. The construction worker cooperatives should be formed across the states in all the local areas with the investment or shareholding from local people and the workers themselves. One per state, county or district linked to the federal cooperative which brings all the state and local cooperatives together. All the technology and support required to manage the whole construction cooperative will be provided by the technology and support cooperative. The investment required in the cooperative is not millions and billions as being projected by the bankers and financiers to deter workers from creating cooperatives but, only a fraction (around 10%) of the all the projects which they can do. The rest (90%) will be financed at low interest from government or banks. The notion of huge capital requirement for these projects is false and misleading to deter construction workers and ordinary people from forming cooperatives and benefitting.

20

LEGAL-JUSTICE FOR ALL

Like healthcare, legal problems are the reason for many bankruptcies and financial ruin for many people. A simple civil case for a land dispute between the families itself would take years to resolve with hundreds of visits to the court. It is a dreaded problem faced by people and a drain on their finances. Most of the money is wasted in endless cases and unending trips to courts all over the world. In most cases, justice is gained by the one who has more money and who has sustaining power.

The criminal justice system also is helping the rich and the poor and the uneducated are always denied justice and incarcerated in most countries. Most conveniently, the capitalist system has separated the justice system dealing with the financial frauds into white-collar crimes which are only punishable by fines rather than prison terms. This explains why the financial crimes which led to the crash of 2008 financial system did not see a single person go to prison. It is time people recognize these crimes which devastate the lives of millions of people financially and ensure they are given the same treatment as the thefts and other criminal cases.

The US has almost 2.4 million people in prisons. The system is completely against the poor. A person who cannot post the bail money lingers in jail for years. Covid-19 has seen many inmates contracting the virus, but the system is not capable of taking care of the people in prison. This is also due to the ridiculous system of private prisons in the US. Private prisons? Really? It is preposterous. There are stories about prisoners being denied bail, due to the contract between the prison management and the government which requires a minimum number of prisoners required in a private prison. The people who are in prison for possession of marijuana are still lingering in prison even when many states legalized marijuana. The prison and incarceration of the poor, while the so-called white-collar criminals are fined for their mega frauds, is the example of the corporatization of the legal justice system.

The recent amendments in India to the UAPA (Unlawful Activities Prevention Act) is to facilitate speedy investigation and prosecution in terror-related offences. The most important part of it is allowing an individual to be designated as a terrorist, a measure that is in line with the global practices. These are laws made and open to misuse by governments and to keep the citizens in check with the fear of an invisible enemy.

There is a need for a complete overhaul of the system and the new system will consider it with an organized approach rather than as an individual. People-organizations created specifically for human rights, legal rights and other issues will be able to change the system. Also, considering the importance of the courts and justice system as the third pillar of democracy, the people-organization overseeing it is necessary.

The lawyers and law profession should be subscription-based like the media. All the citizens have representation with a small fee they pay per year to protect themselves from the unnecessary burden of prolonged cases and unjust incarceration. The orientation, counselling and out-of-court settlements should be prioritized and court cases should be the last resort. The subscription model for lawyers' fees will help cases to be settled amicably out of court and help the law professionals.

The courts and justice system require technology tools to efficiently manage the cases. In India, we can see overcrowded courts with people with cases sitting for hours together just waiting for the case to be called. Even lawyers are wasting their time waiting when they can be doing productive work. The delays and postponement of cases are common, and the defendants come to know only in the last moment when they have reached the court. A simple messaging system would help enormously in waste of time and money for many people. There are several technology tools available or can be developed to help the courts and cases in the new economic system. Some of them are:

1. Information management system and app for court cases and schedules

2. Tele-conferencing to avoid unnecessary travel to the courts

3. Digitization of records and acceptance of digitized records

4. Subscription model for legal support

21

Sports and Games

For many people, Sports and Arts are hobby and passion. Even though in many cases, it is pursued in spare time, it is an industry and generates huge income and financial gains to only a few. Any industry which generates wealth and financial gains should provide employment and financial gains to many. For the people who play sports professionally, support as coaches, caddies and many other professions, it is not equitable income. Only a few make most of the money and the others struggle. The people who associate themselves with the sports (but are not sportspeople nor support-people like the club owners, managers and equipment-manufacturers and marketers), make more money than the sportspeople on an average. The income to sports is generated mostly by the spectators and fans who are paying a bigger and bigger penalty for their pastime. This is one industry which requires a collective and cooperative approach.

The caddies in one of the prestigious golf courses in Bangalore, India, are working at the course for many years. Some of them have worked there for more than 10 years. There are about 50 caddies every day and the number goes up to 150 on the weekends. The working means they just show up every day but may or may not get work as they do not get any salary or perks. Forget perks, they do not get food or water also from the management. The only income is from the golfer's caddie-fee and if the golfers feed them at the turn. If the golfers do not show up, the caddies don't get any work or income. Many caddies work for the love of the game, but this system where the owners of the golf course benefit without giving due payment to the caddies who are an integral part of a golf course is regrettable. The caddies' thinking of forming association or union is not going to solve the problem. What they need is a cooperative which provides them with income from not just caddying, but from other activities like sale of equipment or accessories, etc. This is the case in many sports where even as professionals, they do not make enough to make a career out of it. If the sport, in general, is not making any money, it is excusable, but, when there is so much revenue available from the professional events, it is time everyone involved get an equitable income from it.

Sports and games are the biggest examples of 99% and 1% divide. 99% of the athletes struggle and less than one percent gain huge dividends from their talent. India, a country of more than billion people obsessed with cricket which can only accommodate 11 players in their team, while there may be more than a million players who aspire to be in the Indian cricket team. The percentage of success is less than that of winning a lottery, but hundreds of thousands still try for it. We have to wonder what happens to all those players who did not make it and instead of pursuing their passion, have to do some other job which they hate all their life. Similar cases are there in the USA and other parts of the world where only a few out of millions make the cut to be professionals and the rest just fade away.

This inequality is also caused by the capitalists who see it as a money-making scheme and muddy the water for everyone. The football leagues, cricket leagues and all other sports leagues have only financial intentions and have no love for sports. The ticket prices for all these professional events have increased exponentially while the wages remain stagnant for most of us. The frenzy of competitiveness has made the sports-watching miserable to most of us as one team of individuals can win and the rest of them will lose. The prize money for the winners is increased to exploit the athletes to strive for more and more glory. With this kind of pressure and financial gains, the athletes are made to cheat and face the consequences alone instead of the system which drove them to it.

The new system should be athletes-driven and everyone involved in the sports should be benefitted with the professional events, equipment, sportswear, ticket sales and government spending on sports. This can happen when the organizations are formed of fans, athletes and others related to people and also by building the cooperatives of sports-related people to take control of the sports. The new system will provide all the technology and support required to establish these organizations and collectives to further the interest of sportspeople.

22

SOCIAL AND PUBLIC SECTOR

The concept of social and public (political) work being voluntary and people with passion doing the work is wrong. With most of the working people struggling to maintain their families, the only people who will go into social and public service would be the ones who have money and no day-to-day problems. This is the reason we see unqualified and corrupt people in politics. Social service is not just people doing voluntarily, but will be a very good career option for many people who enjoy doing this work. The NGOs, associations and social organizations are doing a lot of work, but it is not attracting the kind of people who really want to do dedicated service, but cannot due to the financial constraints. Also, the organizations remain confined to local areas due to lack of technology tools and professional managers who can take these organizations to the next level.

The new system has recognized the problem and economic systems like capitalism and socialism work best in democratically elected governments. When there was a need for a capitalistic form of the economic system, the state would act as a referee to avoid unequal distribution of wealth. If the capitalists (investors) take more from the system, the tax system would reflect the excess and redistribute in terms of welfare and other programmes to make it a more equal society. However, the cycle was broken when the capitalists started influencing the government and capturing the bigger pie from the economic system.

The tag of job creators was given by them to themselves and all kinds of subsidies, freebies and many giveaways taken from the government as well as reducing the taxes to the lowest level for the investors and corporates. This skewed financial flow in favour of the corporates has led to the inequality seen today.

This collusion between the elected officials and the corporates reflects in the election results across the globe in India, Russia and finally now in the United States. The corporates finance the elections to both or all parties which are contesting to make sure that no matter who wins, they are the beneficiaries. The people are left in the lurk with the powerful monies influencing the democracies around the world.

It is also unfortunate that the elected representatives have become the kings. The so-called leaders have forgotten the mandate and the representation that the people have chosen them. However, it is only because we let them be the kings. The elected representatives make their own rules and disappear from the people who elected them for the term and people don't care to make them accountable. This is the problem with the existing democracies and it is time to refine it and make it work for everyone.

The two-party system in the US is a problem, but the multi-party system in India is a bigger problem. It is because, like capitalism, the parties are created by demigods who have only their interest in mind and try to sway the party in that direction. The party manifesto would be created only during elections and candidates are selected (or join) conveniently only during the election. The people have no idea about the candidates and candidates have not worked for the people before the election. For a democracy to work, its political parties should start as a grass-root organization with a mandate and manifesto in mind. The candidates or representatives should work on the mandate for a certain period of time before they would get the opportunity to be the representatives.

The basic structure of the party which represents the people should be the party made by the people, funded by the people and managed by the people, without the interference of the special interest groups and corporates. Democracy is for the people only and never for the entities created by the people. If any decision, bill or legislation is to be passed it should consider only the interest of the people. Both the government and the corporates are creations of people and only people should decide how they need to be run.

The democratic process of electing the government in the new system should start with the organizations of people. Like most of the other organizations, faiths, or marginalized communities and poor, the people-organizations are important to make sure that all the communities are represented and have their representatives to protect their interest. It is normal in a democracy that the majority rules all the time. But, if there are representatives from each community based on the population, it is the just system for all people. Also, the representative should only execute the manifesto prepared by the people and people would have the final say. If most people want single-payer or universal healthcare, that is what should be implemented without questioning the will of the people. With the advent of technology, there is a precise way to get votes on specific issues rather than trying to take skewed polls and making decisions. The people can vote electronically which would ensure 100% voting on issues which matter.

The idea of the election process is completely misrepresented in all democratic countries. The expectation of a person who is elected as a 'leader' rather than a representative is that he knows more than the folks who elect him. Once elected, he is supposed to go and legislate laws on his own accord. That is totally opposite of what is required by a representative. It does not happen in any other profession. What if a teacher, once employed, decides to do his own way of teaching instead of what is there in the curriculum. Or a president of an organization has his own agenda than that of one of the members he is representing? This trend must be broken, and the representative should follow the agenda given to them by the people and no other bias should be allowed by them.

Government policies

Government policy for the industrial sector, region or communities should be purely based on the welfare of the people rather than the corporates. The corporate organizations have found it easy to influence the policies by lobbying and other means to create government rules, regulations and policies based on their needs. The influence of corporate and private entities is seen in every policy made by governments around the world. The Trump administration has systematically dismantled or weakened all the departments and regulations which were working for the interest of people. The citizens of the United States are mute spectators while the whole system is turned upside-down by him. Even though it is not a new phenomenon the American people are witnessing, the profound way it is being done is new. It is not his fault that he is doing these, but it is the fault of the American people who let this be done. A few sporadic protests will not change the system and it must be done at the systemic level where the people whom we elect to represent do not work for corporates but for the people. If these things are to happen, grass-root organizations at every level should be created and define the agenda for the representatives to follow rather the corporates doing it now.

Around the world, there is a majority-minority bias in one way or other. In the USA, there is a huge difference in economic development based on race. The African Americans, Hispanics and Native Americans are marginalized communities in social, political and economic development. In India, the caste-based discrimination has the backward castes (Scheduled Castes/Scheduled Tribes), Muslims and to some extent, Christians marginalized. The vote-bank politics of India has left these community votes divided among the major parties which use them to their benefit and keep them suppressed when it comes to social and economic development. This trend is everywhere, and the corporatization and automation have affected these marginalized communities more than any other community. While the Everything-People model does take all people as one, these marginalized communities require special attention and additional support to make them self-sufficient first and bring to the mainstream.

The problems in each country with the marginalized communities may be different, but in general, the following solutions will help in tackling the problems specific to their communities.

1. Organizing to have a voice to represent the whole community as one in social, political and economic development

2. Taking full advantage of government policy provided to get the maximum benefits

3. Using technology to the community benefit

4. Education and training support to be competitive in the job market

5. Healthcare support for the stress-free development

6. Cooperative businesses providing jobs and additional income

The new economic system would provide all the technology tools and support required to create these organizations, provide the knowledge support to identify and undo and correct every policy which is working against the interest of the people.

CONCLUSION

The new economic system proposed is not limited to the sectors highlighted in this book, rather a starting point for many more ideas from people around the world to make it a completely people-centric world. System changes proposed in this book are not based on my wild imaginations and dreams, rather a practical possibility which the people around the world should take and run with it.

I know the questions which readers of my book would be asking. How do we start? What next? etc. Well, the first step would be to find one people-organization to join or start a people-organization to bring people together and from there the system will take shape by itself. Without organization, there is no new system and no solution.

The technology emphasis is the most important aspect of this book. My experience with the people past 50 is of scepticism and absolute disdain for technology. Also, most people outside the technology realm consider it to be expensive and cannot afford it. But it is not true, and I have developed many technology tools required to implement this new economic system and will be made available to people-organizations through this book's website *everythingpeople.org*.

The cooperative system discussed is one major aspect that needs to be understood by people. The present-day cooperatives do not represent even remotely the cooperatives I am talking about. Again, technology plays a big role in shaping the new cooperatives. We have a lot of resources and help in establishing the new-age cooperatives and professionally manage to be more effective.

This is not an end of learning, but just the beginning of a long journey which cannot be taken by one person or a small group of people. It is the journey I am willing to take along with every one of you. Are you ready?

I have established a foundation **Everything-People foundation** which will be an organization to help implementation of the systems talked about in this book. Some of the book-royalty from this book will go to the foundation.

My company Phapa technology which was established in 2018-19 along with my friend Tareque Pirzada has developed technology tools and system for organizations for people in general and to help unorganized workers to facilitate them social security and welfare benefits, skill-development, jobs, etc. These tools will be available to Everything-People organizations to help in organizing people.

You may be interested to know why a person who talks so much about people-organizations and cooperatives throughout this book has a private company. Even though it is a registered private company, it is a social enterprise with social support using technology to get social security and welfare benefits to the unorganized, migrant, gig-economy and low-wage workers. I did try to establish a technology-cooperative to develop the technologies required for the new economic system three years ago but, people were not ready for it and the bureaucratic system in India is so bad that there is no way a legitimate cooperative business can be established in the present system. There is a huge policy change to be made to the cooperative system. These are the problems I faced and the Everything-People-organization will make sure they are addressed and help people to form cooperatives and thrive.

First, the state cooperative department refused to register a cooperative which is going to work as a technology company. They thought I was trying to scam people and run away by collecting Rs.2300 per person, the share application money.

Next, they put a condition that I have to go and get 1000 shareholders willing to pay Rs. 2300 per head. And a total capital of Rs.20,00,000. And the director constantly suggested that "Why you are hell-bent on a cooperative when you can start a private company with two people and Rs.100,000 capital?" I did succeed in convincing 400 people, but only about 100 could pay. After one year of struggle, I had to return the money and started the private company and put off the technology-cooperative for a later date. But, one day, I will establish a technology-cooperative as a model for the new economic system.

It is not easy to fight the system alone. With this book, I want the people of the world to open their minds to the wonderful possibilities beyond the capitalistic system. Everything-People organizations will work towards organizing the unorganized and providing the necessary support for people-organizations to be established and succeed.

www.ingramcontent.com/pod-product-compliance
Lightning Source LLC
Chambersburg PA
CBHW030639220526
45463CB00004B/1585